The Lygons of Madresfield Court

The Lygons of Madresfield Court

by
Dorothy E. Williams

Logaston Press

LOGASTON PRESS
Little Logaston, Logaston,
Woonton, Almeley, Herefordshire HR3 6QH

First published by Logaston Press 2001
Copyright © text Dorothy E. Williams 2001 (with © of the relevant documents
belonging to Madresfield Court remaining with the owner of Madresfield Court)
© of illustrations as acknowledged in the Acknowledgements

All rights reserved. No part of this publication
may be reproduced, stored in a retrieval system,
or transmitted, in any form or by any means,
electronic, mechanical, photocopying, recording
or otherwise, without the prior permission,
in writing of the publisher

ISBN 1 873827 32 6

Set in Times and Baskerville by Logaston Press
and printed in Great Britain by
The Cromwell Press, Trowbridge

Front cover: The courtyard at Madresfield Court in 1889

Contents

		page
	Acknowledgements	*vi*
	Introduction	*vii*
Chapter I	Obscure Origins	1
Chapter II	Enter the Beauchamps and the Lygons	5
Chapter III	William the Correspondent	13
Chapter IV	Waiting for a New Dawn	19
Chapter V	William Lygon, First Earl Beauchamp (1747-1816)	25
Chapter VI	William, Second Earl Beauchamp (1782-1823)	37
Chapter VII	John Reginald (Lygon) Pindar, Third Earl Beauchamp (1783-1853)	49
Chapter VIII	Henry, Fourth Earl Beauchamp (1785-1863)	53
Chapter IX	Henry, Fifth Earl Beauchamp (1829-1866)	69
Chapter X	Frederick, Sixth Earl Beauchamp (1830-1891)	77
Chapter XI	William, Seventh Earl Beauchamp (1872-1938)	99
Chapter XII	William, Eighth Earl Beauchamp (1903-1979)	121
	Bibliography	125
	Index	127

Acknowledgements

The author acknowledges with gratitude the help received from many sources, in particular the following: Lady Rosalind Morrison and the Trustees of the Madresfield Estate for their continued interest and support in allowing her to use the extensive resources of the Madresfield archives; staff at Birmingham City Library, Worcester City Library, especially Malvern Public Library; and County Record Offices at Hereford, Gloucester and Worcester, who have all been unfailingly patient and helpful; Dr Diana McClatchey for much information regarding the development of women's ministry in the Church of England; Dr Tania Rose for sharing her extensive research into certain aspects of the seventh earl's political career; members of the Passionist Order, especially Fr. Ignatius at Broadway, Worcestershire, and Fr. Bernard Lowe, Provincial Superior at Mount Argus, Dublin, for facilitating reserach into the life of Fr. Paul Mary (Charles R. Pakenham), and for permitting quotations from the official biography; and individual correspondents, too numerous to list, who have often helped to clarify an obscure point.

The story of a family so long established is inevitably bound to have collected a number of legends, or at least unsubstantiated traditions, and consequently in order to avoid perpetuating hearsay it has been necessary to omit the occasional 'pretty' or 'scandalous' tale. The aim has been to include only those matters which it has been possible to verify.

Logaston Press wishes to thank Lady Morrison for the illustrations on pages 3, 9, 26, 27, 33, 44, 51, 57, 61, 62, 63, 72, 80, 82, 89, 94, 115 and 117, and the Rector of Madresfield and the churchwardens for providing access to the church.

Introduction

Madresfield in Worcestershire lies at the foot of the Malvern Hills, visible from the higher reaches but otherwise well hidden from the casual observer even now. When Malvern Chase was preserved for the King's hunting, the forest helped to obscure the hamlet, and today only the spire of its Victorian church indicates its location amongst the farmlands on the outskirts of Malvern town. Madresfield Court is itself tucked away from the village.

If there were a Premier League of Stately Homes, based on points awarded for size of house and fame/notoriety of its owners past or present, Madresfield might not qualify. But if the criteria were changed to antiquity of site and length of owners' lineage, there would be a startling alteration in such a league. For beneath Madresfield Court are the foundations of an Anglo-Saxon building, and the honour of having received the first grant of arms from an English monarch, in 1170, was shared between the Longspee Earls of Salisbury and the Beauchamps of Warwick.

But Madresfield is a treasure in its own right. Despite two periods when the future of the Court seemed very uncertain, it has survived to the present day, greatly changed but with one outstanding link through 800 years of recorded history: since its original owners it has never been sold or passed into other hands except by inheritance, and in some respects the history of the building mirrors the story of the family. Yet, whilst one can classify architecture by easily recognisable periods or styles, a family is a collection of individuals. They are not merely names and dates in a chronological account, but people who lived and loved, sometimes hated, occasionally intrigued, but above all were human just like the rest of us, and Madresfield Court was their home. Even today, when it appears in lists of Stately Homes worthy of a visit, the ethos is that of a home rather than a show place.

Most of the records for Madresfield's first six centuries or so are confined to legal documents; the archives contain well over 12,000 deeds. But from the time of the William Lygon who lived from 1642 to 1721 and who left a collection of some 800 letters, we have the means for a closer acquaintance with the family. For the next 250 years there are letters of Lygon family members ranging from, in one case, just a handful to thousands in the correspondence of the sixth and seventh earls.

The deeds record the increasing Lygon landholdings and reflect the increasing levels of importance of members of the family. Unlike many families who chose warfare to make their name, the law proved more popular with the Lygons, each generation producing one or two lawyers. Rather oddly, in spite of the Beauchamp patronage of religion throughout the centuries, very few chose the Church as their vocation until the middle of Victoria's reign. But for the most part they seem to have lived on their estates, becoming sheriffs, magistrates, merchants and agriculturists. They looked after their tenants—yeomen farmers and tradesmen such as blacksmiths and millers—perhaps, to a modern mind, in an unacceptably paternalistic way.

The book notes the sequence of events at the Court, but its main endeavour is to tell the story of the family whose members have each contributed to the magic of Madresfield. The family motto *Fortuna mea in bello campo* was taken from Psalm 16, verse 7 in Cranmer's translation: 'The lot is fallen unto me in a fair ground; yea, I have a goodly heritage'. It is indeed a goodly heritage.

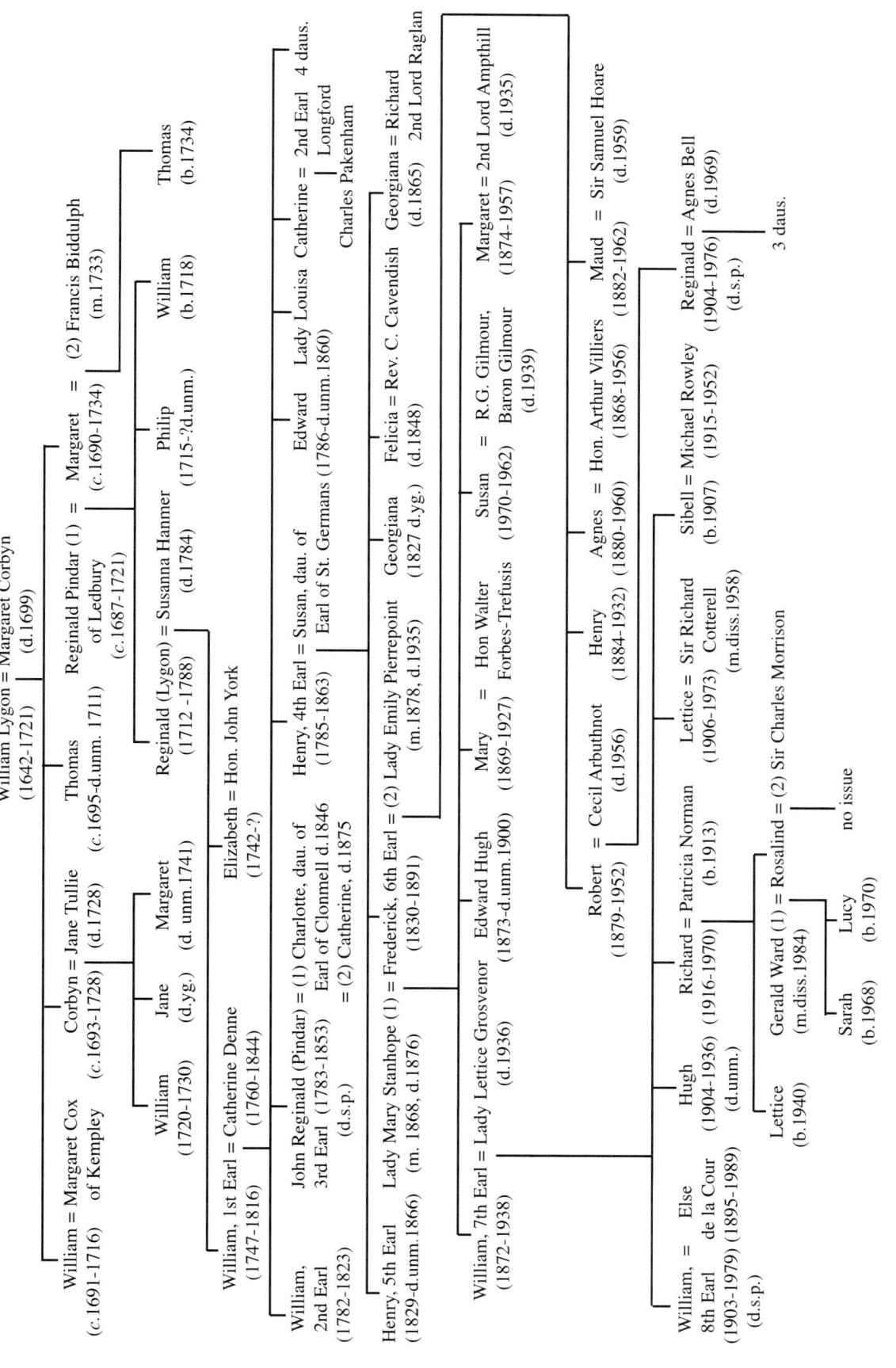

The Lygon Family (since 1642)

An extract from the first accounts for provisioning the Star Chamber with wine from Gascony after the accession of James I of England, records held at Madresfield Court

CHAPTER ONE
Obscure Origins

Madresfield does not appear in Domesday, but the evidence of Anglo-Saxon foundations discovered at the Court in the 19th century, and of Anglo-Saxon derivation for several local place-names, indicate the presence of a settlement here before the Norman Conquest. The name 'Madresfield' is, however, included in a cartulary known as the 'Westminster Doomsday' which dates from 1086. Brian Smith in *A History of Malvern* considers this may indicate a Roman origin, though the seventh Earl Beauchamp (1872-1938) preferred an Anglo-Saxon derivation from Maedhre's (a Saxon forename) field.

As early as the 9th century B.C. Bronze Age man left axe-heads here as a memento of his presence, whilst Iron Age or Celtic man formed the British Camp on the nearby Malvern Hills, but it is with the Romans that evidence of local settlement starts to emerge. Roman coins have been found in the vicinity of Madresfield Court, and there are suggestions that the hamlet may have been used as a staging post for the Roman army on its way from Worcester to the Malvern Hills. Roman tiles have also been unearthed in several places in this area.

Whilst the antiquity of Madresfield's origins can be seen as an asset, it is also a liability, for to some extent one has to rely on tradition to supply the earlier details, whilst the chronicler of a later date has official records to consult. In Madresfield Court there are a number of 'pedigree charts', or family trees, as these documents are now called, which purport to show the descent of the family from various historical figures of great antiquity, but our main authority is that which was approved by the College of Heralds when the revival of the Beauchamp title was granted in 1806, and, as amended in the individual grant of arms, to each new holder of the title since. There is also a very large pedigree chart, believed to have been the work of the seventh Earl Beauchamp, a keen genealogist and an excellent calligrapher. His study was as extensive as the inherent limitation of existing records allowed, and providing that this caveat is borne in mind, his account is an invaluable aid to the history of the family. Written records also start within 50 years of the Norman Conquest, showing that at least two, and probably three, descendants of Norman knights were to become owners of what was evidently a much-prized property.

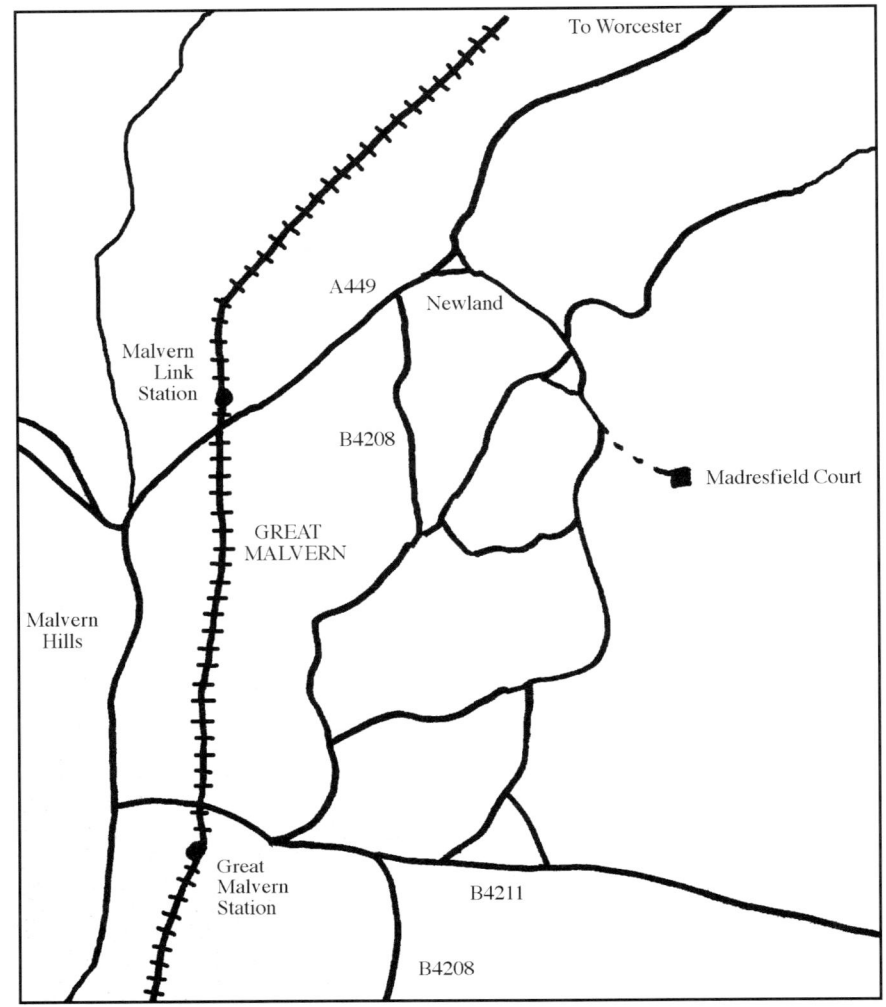
Map (not to scale) showing the location of Madresfield Court

The Westminster cartulary of 1086 records that Madresfield was in the possession of Urse d'Abitot, the famous Sheriff of Worcestershire and local tradition has it that he gave it as his daughter's dowry when she was married to a Norman knight. This was presumably a de Braci, for a de Braci 'of Worcestershire' is noted in 1168, a William de Bracy is similarly identified in 1176 and by 1196 Robert de Bracy was 'of Madresfield' when the hamlet had official recognition and its own church, a tiny stone building with a thatched roof and a pyramidal spire close to the entrance to the present Court.

In the 1990s a planning application was made in connection with the development of a small portion of Madresfield Estate for residential and commercial use. During the protracted discussions which followed, one hitherto unrecognised landmark was pinpointed: a ditch approximately four metres wide, bounded on either side by ancient oak and wild service trees. Two independent panels of experts estimated this to be at least 800 years old, dating from when it was probably part of the original western boundary of the estate and manor. It may well be that either William or Robert de Bracy was responsible for planting this hedge, for in 1170 a de Bracy was one of those mentioned in Henry II's charter for the building of a priory at Malvern. Although de Bracy may have felt it politic to support the king's patronage for a new foundation at Malvern, he must also have been aware of the Church's reputation for land acquisition—Domesday shows that already 64% of Worcestershire was then in ecclesiastical ownership. De Bracy's lands were bounded by the enormous sprawling parish of Powyke on one side and the monks of Worcester Cathedral on the other, whose lands stretched from Malvern to the Severn at Clevelode.

In such circumstances and in the absence of detailed records and often clear delineation of boundaries, he may well have felt it advisable to mark his territory permanently and unmistakably. This ditch has been preserved and can be seen (OS 4738 7959) on the northern side of Townsend Way, just a few metres south of the roundabout that gives access to Spring Lane.

In due course Madresfield became what has been described as 'an island of independence in an ecclesiastical sea', an independence reinforced by the fact that the small church of St. Mary, although eventually listed in diocesan records, was to remain for some centuries effectively the private chapel of the Court, served by the family's chaplain and used principally by its owners, employees and tenants. For most of the 16th century—about the time of the Reformation—it was supplemented by a small chapel dedicated to St. Mary Magdalene at nearby Lower Woodsfield, also on the estate, where the monks at Newland (a Novice Master and two novices) were allowed to say Mass once a week, possibly as part of the novices' training.

The manor of Madresfield remained in the ownership of the de Bracy line for some three centuries. They were evidently loyal servants of the king, frequently mentioned in the usual appointments to various commissions in the county or as justices of the peace. The most unfavourable mention is of a Sir Robert de Bracy who on several occasions from 1333 to 1354 was charged with hunting not only in the royal chase at Malvern, but also in

What Madresfield Court was to become. An aerial view in the 1990s

the bishop's park at Blockley. On one occasion he was accompanied by 'the parson of Madresfield'; it is not clear whether this aggravated or lessened the offence. However, none of this interfered with his public service, not even as a justice of the peace.

The de Bracy line ended with William, who married Isabel (family name unknown), by whom he had a daughter, Joan; no other children are recorded. William de Bracy died some time before 1450. Joan de Bracy married, before 1423, Thomas Lygon, a member of a family who already owned extensive lands in Worcestershire, Warwickshire, Shropshire and possibly Herefordshire. He also died some time before 1450 leaving, apparently, only one son, William. Isabel de Bracy, Joan's widowed mother, who was still alive, then demised by a deed in 1450 her manor of Madresfield to her grandson William Lygon, so in due course bringing to Madresfield's ownership the surname which has ever since been associated with the Court. By this deed she reserved to herself part of the house for her own occupation for her lifetime. She seems to have died about 1456, probably then over 70 years of age, and the ownership of Madresfield passed to the line of Lygon, the surname which has ever since been associated with the Court.

CHAPTER TWO
Enter the Beauchamps and the Lygons

The Lygons were themselves of ancient lineage. The name is certainly of French origin, and they were the holders of properties in Worcester city, as well as extensive lands in the surrounding counties. Before the end of the 15th century all the Lygon lands, through inheritance, had been absorbed into the Madresfield estate. The first 'Lygon of Madresfield' was the William mentioned in the last chapter. In 1495 there is a reference to Thomas Lygon, about five years after his son Richard had married Anne Beauchamp, a union which is a significant indication of the standing both of Lygon and Madresfield.

Anne Beauchamp 'of Powyke' traced her ancestry back to William Beauchamp, Lord of Elmley Castle and hereditary castellan of Worcester, an office which had come to this family after the eclipse of the d'Abitots. Anne's was a long lineage going back to before the Norman Conquest. The Beauchamps of Powyke were descended from the first Beauchamp of Warwick whose grant of arms in 1170 along with those of the original Longespee earls of Salisbury, were the first ever granted by an English sovereign. Her grandfather, John Beauchamp, was a younger son of the Warwick family who was rewarded with the title 'Baron Beauchamp of Powyke' in consideration of his service to Henry VI and his father, Henry V. He was Master of the king's horses, Lieutenant and Treasurer of the Isle of Wight, Knight of the Garter and—inevitably—the holder of immense areas of land, especially in central England. He was one of those sent by Henry VI to negotiate with Richard of York at Dartford in 1452, attended parliaments in both 1459 and 1461 and meetings of the council in between times in 1460. He appears to have taken no part in the fighting during the Wars of the Roses, perhaps due to old age or because his talents lay simply in administration.

He supported the friars, although whether he particularly favoured the Augustinian or Dominican order is unclear, and is credited with having been a prime mover in the introduction of friars to Worcestershire. When he died in 1474, Worcester saw one of its worst riots between monks and friars. Indeed, to have been associated with their introduction was a doubtful honour. The monks at Worcester Cathedral and Malvern Priory strongly objected to anyone intruding on what they perceived as their territory, both material and spiritual, and the friars undermined the relationship of the monks with the common people. Hitherto, the monks had had control over all religious practice and, above all, great influence as to the use of their parishioners' finances. A contemporary chronicler, Matthew of Westminster, himself a monk, expresses their view neatly: 'O sorrow, O more than sorrow, O vicious pestilence. The Friars Minor have come to England ... Neither were they slack in assisting the sick to make their wills, which employment did not a little hinder the monks both in point of profit and power.'

But John Beauchamp, until then a generous patron of Worcester Cathedral, apparently attempted to be equally generous with the friars to whom he gave land near the cathedral so that they might build a church, and in fact he seems to have wanted to be buried there in due course. It was not allowed to happen. There had already been an occasion when a 'defector's' coffin had been seized by the monks, for possession of the corpse and its subsequent burial was vital to the success of claimants to his possessions; for instance, in the case of a knight, his best horse, complete with the owner's finest suit of armour, could be claimed by those who interred his body. These disorderly scenes were repeated in the case of John, first Baron Beauchamp of Powyke and the monks at first buried him in the apparently disused vegetable garden of the cathedral, although when the building was later extended this was included within its walls and its location subsequently lost.

John Beauchamp of Powyke left only one son, Richard (*c*.1434-1502/3), who inherited the title and all the lands, but apparently took no part in public affairs. However, he in his turn left three daughters, between whom in due course all his property was divided.

To Anne, the second daughter, was given the large and important Manor of Powyke, as well as the ancient Beauchamp's Court at Callow End, a few miles from Madresfield, along with many other properties in both the city and county of Worcester—a very considerable addition to the already extensive lands of the Lygons when she married Richard Lygon. Most of these lands remained intact within the ownership of the head of the Lygon family throughout the following centuries, not only because they were often entailed but also because younger Lygon sons were frequently given a lump sum with which to build their own fortunes, and occasionally a small annuity. Daughters received a generous dowry on marriage. If they remained unmarried their future was more uncertain; sometimes careful provision was made, but such annuities were not usually popular with the new owner.

Perhaps it was the introduction of the Beauchamp genes into the Lygon family which accounts for the longevity of their female descendants, for despite the perils of childbirth exacerbated by large families, there are in the Lygon family some outstanding examples, daughters usually outliving their brothers. For example, Anne's great-grandfather, Walter de Beauchamp, who died in 1303, left a widow, Alice, who must then have been at least 40 years old and already the mother of a large family. But about six years later she departed on a pilgrimage 'beyond the seas'. We do not know how far she travelled, but four years later she was home again and taking a large part in the management of various manors in Beauchamp jurisdiction. In 1329 she shrewdly settled the manor of Mutton on her son Giles in return for an annuity for her life of £100, then a very large sum. Twenty years later she was still alive, when she must have been more than 80 years old. One hopes her son's filial devotion was not diminished by the longevity of his mother and her annuity.

Anne Lygon presented an altar dedicated to the Magi to the church built by friars on, it is believed, the site now occupied by Laslett's Almshouses in Worcester city, as a memorial to her grandparents John and Margaret Beauchamp. She also provided for Madresfield's tiny first church a stained glass window 'In memory of Augustine Simmonds'. It is not known who Simmonds was; possibly a friar, for the window showed a kneeling figure in a black habit, perhaps one whose order had been introduced by her grandfather to Worcestershire; black habits were worn by Augustinian and Dominican orders. If Simmonds was a friar, he would have been totally dependent on the family at the Court, for one of the complaints of the monks against the friars was that the latter, belonging to no static community, relied entirely on charity for their upkeep, so diminishing donations to other causes. Nor did bishops necessarily welcome the permanent presence of friars in the diocese, for in the absence of other means of support maintenance of a friar could become the bishop's personal responsibility. No doubt Worcester's bishop was relieved when Simmonds became the responsibility of the Lygons at Madresfield, presumably as chaplain.

Anne Lygon's story is somewhat similar to the story of her Beauchamp ancestress related above, except for the pilgrimage overseas. She had eight sons (no daughters are mentioned), was over 40 years of age when her husband, Richard, died in 1512, and survived him by 22 years. Her eldest son, also Richard, on inheriting the estates, settled on her the manor of Bradwell together with rents accruing from another, so that she too, like Alice Beauchamp nearly two centuries earlier, could lead an independent life. The sons all shared in the income from the estates, with the exception of one son, George, a priest who was therefore ineligible to inherit. Other sons left Madresfield to live in London, Gloucestershire or Herefordshire. Michael, who lived at Beauchamp's Court in Callow End, for nearly 50 years, had six sons, scattered throughout the counties of Worcester, Gloucester, Hereford and Somerset. But although it might be supposed that this was the start of a vast network of Lygons, this did not in the long run prove to be the case; eventually the name was perpetuated only to some extent in Gloucester, London and of course at Madresfield.

Anne's eldest son Richard acquired, on his marriage to Margery Grevell c.1510, the property of Arle Court, near Cheltenham, where he continued to live until his mother's death in 1534. One gains the impression, strengthened in the centuries which followed, of what has been called 'a dominant female', not in every generation, but certainly there have been many women who have exercised a profound influence, usually for good, on the family's fortunes.

Richard had four sons and five daughters, of whom fortunately only one, never marrying, required an annuity. Knighted on the coronation of Anne Boleyn, Henry VIII's second wife, in 1532, when he was sheriff of Gloucestershire, Richard served in 1544 in the war with France, and in 1548-9 was sheriff of Worcestershire. The acquisition of Arle

Court, which had a number of manors attached, resulted in further settlements of the family in Gloucestershire.

The trauma of the Reformation had a comparatively mild effect on Madresfield, which even then lived in a world of its own. Worship in its tiny chapel went on untroubled; unlike many churches Madresfield was never forced to accept the ministry of priests not episcopally ordained, and, as a rector noted with satisfaction in the 1930s 'Here for 620 years the Apostolic Succession has remained unbroken'. In this respect probably the Beauchamp connection proved most useful. As the descendants of Anne (Beauchamp) Lygon, that devoted daughter and benefactress of the Church, the Madresfield family must have been acceptable to Queen Mary, for when Richard's son, William, succeeded him he was able to offer in 1557 with impunity the position of Chaplain at Madresfield to Thomas Gylham, a secular priest from St. Thomas's, the original parish church of Malvern (which stood on the site of the present Post Office close to Malvern Priory). Gylham had been too eager, as soon as legislation allowed such clergy to marry, to enter into matrimony at once and so lost his living within a short space of time once Mary became Queen. But William Lygon took him, and presumably his bride, to Madresfield. Gylham remained at Madresfield for four years, when he moved to another parish after his patron's death, but again the Madresfield post was filled by a priest left homeless by the suppression of the monasteries.

William married, whilst still under age, Eleanor, daughter of Sir William Denys of Gloucestershire. The marriage contract had one or two notable stipulations: The respective parents had to provide clothing for their offspring appropriate to their standing in society, and the father of the bride had also to provide living accommodation for her as long as not only her prospective mother-in-law but also her grandmother-in-law was alive. This suggests that William's relations were perhaps not altogether welcoming to the bride. Be that as it may, William and Eleanor had a family of seven sons and four daughters.

The Madresfield family are frequently typical of their time, including their religious allegiances, and this is particularly apparent in this generation. One son, Fernando, showed his uncertainty by at first seeking service under Nicholas Heath, the then Roman Catholic Archbishop of York. Unsuccessful in this, he turned to those who were plotting the removal of Mary and the installation of Elizabeth as queen. Although he was arrested, he managed to allay suspicions, and next appears in command of 300 arquebusiers on the Scottish borders. In 1559 he was in the service of Henry, Lord Berkeley, in Gloucestershire, whose wife was his aunt, and after that he spent the rest of his life on one of the family estates at Arle. Like his brothers, he had been left an annuity of £8 from the Madresfield estates.

Another son was Ralph, who was involved in the Duke of Norfolk's plot in 1572 to remove Elizabeth's government. When this failed and the duke was arrested and executed for treason, Ralph left England. In 1574 he was in receipt of a pension from the king of Spain, and the following year went to live in Brussels. In 1577 and 1579 he paid brief visits to England—perhaps to collect his annuity—but next turned up in Flanders and by 1585 was in the employment of the Duke of Parma. In 1605 he again appeared suddenly at Madresfield to collect the arrears of his annuity. The last references to him are in several deeds of 1606.

The next son was Hugh, who was at Oxford in 1568, graduated B.A. in 1570, and went on to become a student at Grays Inn. He remained a Roman Catholic, and is mentioned as a recusant from 1585 onwards. He left London and lived at Hanley Castle with his wife, Barbara, who was also a recusant, until his death in 1601; she died there in 1604.

Richard, William's heir, c.1537-1584, married Mary, daughter of Sir Thomas Russell of Strensham, an association between the two families which was influential for many years to come. They had five sons, of whom three survived. The youngest of these, Henry, proved a somewhat colourful character; he chose the law for his career, and was admitted as a student at the Inner Temple in 1603.

Believed to be Sir William Lygon (c.1563-1608)

Ten years later he killed a barrister of the same Inn in a duel, but he was pardoned in 1620, and retired to live in Powyke where he is said to have died in 1662.

Richard and Mary also had five daughters, and here again the religious divide is apparent. Margaret married Ralph Hornyold and remained a Roman Catholic; Penelope married Robert Walwen/Walweyn, of the prominent Protestant Walweyn family at Newland; and Elizabeth married as his second wife Miles Smyth, Protestant Bishop of Gloucester and one of the translators of the original Authorised Version of the Bible. Two daughters died unmarried.

Sir Richard was succeeded on his death in 1584 by his eldest son William (c.1563-1608), who was just still under age, and two years later married Elizabeth Harewell of

Besford. He was a justice of the peace in 1590, sheriff of Worcestershire 1592-93, knighted by James I in May, 1603, and M.P. for Worcestershire from 1603 to 1608. However, there was more to Sir William's life than such a summary conveys.

He is often called 'William the Wasteful'—not so much to emphasise his somewhat extravagant lifestyle as to distinguish him, coming as he did in the midst of a succession of five Williams who inherited the Court within a 63-year period. He had married before he was 21 and soon ran into financial difficulties, incurring huge debts through somewhat reckless spending and subsequent borrowings, which seem to have been incurred in rebuilding the Court, as much of the remaining fabric of the house is Elizabethan. His great-grandson, the last William of this group, was to blame the impoverished state of Madresfield's finances on his forebear's 'extravagance in great housekeeping' and there are documents in the archives which indicate high levels of expenditure being financed by sales and mortgages. The situation was not helped by his death when his heir was only 18 years of age. In other ways he seems to have maintained his family's tradition of public service.

The third William (1590-1619), being still under age at the time of his father's death, became a ward of the king, and his lands were taken into the custody of the Court of Wards. In due course he was knighted in 1610 and he married the following year Elizabeth Playdell from Gloucestershire. But he died on 30 January, 1619, and once again the Madresfield lands passed into the custody of the Court of Wards.

The fourth William (1613-1681) is the youngest heir to have succeeded to the estates whilst still a child, being just five years old when his father died, leaving him with a brother, John, and a sister, Margaret.

William, as a ward of the king and heir to considerable estates, was at first left in the care of his mother, Dame Elizabeth (Playdell) Lygon, known as Dame Elizabeth the Younger to distinguish her from her mother-in-law Dame Elizabeth (Harewell) Lygon the Elder. The regulations concerning the upbringing of the child show genuine concern for an orphan of such standing. The estates had to be properly administered, but in addition his mother had to covenant to bring up her son 'in good condition, virtuous and decent qualities; and every fourth year as soon as the heir shall be ten years of age, to bring him before the Court of Wards, there to be seen, examined and talked with, in such sort that his manners, education and profiting in learning may be understood and perceived.'

But his grandmother, widow of William the Wasteful, was not prepared to allow his upbringing to be left to his young mother. Her reasons are not recorded, but within 18 months she succeeded in having the custody transferred to herself, and 'banished' her daughter-in-law to live alone at Beauchamp's Court in Callow End, a few miles from Madresfield, with her small daughter and her second son.

Dame Elizabeth the Younger later remarried, to Samuel Knightley, an old friend of the Lygons. He was a London merchant, belonging to a Northamptonshire family, a considerable landowner with a number of London properties, and had a number of links with Worcestershire, including the Devereux family who owned Leigh Sinton Court. He became a good friend to his stepchildren, to whom eventually, having no children of his own, he left much of his property.

When young William reached his majority, there was a long delay and difficulty in obtaining release of his lands from the Court of Wards. Such administrative delays were a common cause for complaint, and this may have been a factor in William's decision to join the Parliamentary Army. Another factor may have been the influence of Samuel Knightley's friendship with several Parliamentarians, though he appears not to have taken an overt part in politics himself. But there is little indication that William had any great enthusiasm for civil war. Although he rose quickly to the rank of colonel, he seems to have been lukewarm in his support—when ordered by Parliament to raze his home to the ground, he somehow omitted to so do.

In 1644 he raised one regiment of horse, but in the following year Madresfield was occupied by the Royalists and he led a siege against its garrison, a siege said to have been lifted in May, 1645, following the surrender of Charles I to the Scots. A year later it was again occupied by Royalists and under siege. On 18 June the Royalist captain, Aston, boasted that he could hold out for three months if necessary, but two or three days later surrendered without a struggle. Colonel Lygon was generous in the terms he offered Captain Aston—£200 for himself, 30s. to each trooper and 10s. for each foot soldier—and is also said to have bought two cannon from Captain Aston, presumably in return for promises not to damage the house or its contents, especially considering William the Wasteful's expenditure. Indeed, the inventory on his own death indicates that the house was very much better furnished than in previous years.

But there is one puzzle which seems impossible to solve. The rectory at Madresfield had been burned down early in the war, and the parochial records lost. Colonel Lygon's family was very young—in 1646 he had certainly two sons and at least one daughter. Where were they when the house was occupied? Probably not at Beauchamp's Court, which was occupied for much of the civil war by Royalists, and the Knightleys were in London; Samuel Knightley wrote in 1647 that he hoped to be back at Beauchamp's Court in 1650.

After the Restoration the colonel was neither fined nor obliged to seek a pardon. The only condition placed upon him was a direction to remain at his country home for the rest of his life, and this was probably no hardship, for his finances were limited. In any case he was evidently a man who was discreet in the expression of his feelings, and he took no further part in public life. He died in 1681.

By his marriage to Mary, daughter of Sir Francis Egiocke, he had six sons. Apart from Richard, who succeeded him, these included William 'the Correspondent' who also inherited Madresfield in due course; Thomas, who became a grocer in London and died unmarried in 1689; Edmund, a barrister of the Middle Temple, and George, who was also a barrister. The last two died before their father, as did the sixth son, Henry, who died in 1666 in his 15th year. William also had four daughters, of whom two died unmarried, and another who died soon after her marriage. The youngest, Anne, married Edward Bull and settled at Hallow Park, near Worcester.

Anne and her husband exercised considerable influence on the fortunes of the Madresfield Lygons. Edward Bull's grandfather was Dr. John Bull the composer. His brother Arundel was a page of the Bedchamber, and in 1660 Edward Bull was appointed 'a yeoman of the standing Wardrobe' to Charles II, an even more intriguing title. Edward Bull speculated in building and had a number of properties in London. Later he developed an interest in tin-mining in Cornwall and became an agent for an official of the Stannaries. After his first wife died and he had remarried to Anne Lygon in 1681, he sold many of his London properties and concentrated on Worcestershire. Their only child died in infancy. They were always on close terms with Madresfield, and their contacts in London proved useful for the future of the colonel's children.

Anne was very close to her brother, the Correspondent, and there are a number of her letters to him in the archives. She had obviously a strong character, and although she would frequently ask his advice, she always made her own decisions, particularly about selling or letting any property. She was also interested in education, especially for the children of the poor—one of her legacies was intended to benefit the children of Madresfield and it still operates almost three centuries later making an annual contribution, (in modern terms now very small), to the needs of the primary school such as in the provision of books and, more recently, computers. She died in 1707, leaving her property at Hallow Park to her niece, Margaret Lygon.

Meanwhile, in 1672, the colonel's eldest son, Richard (?-1687), a barrister of the Middle Temple had married Bridget, daughter of John Lisle of Moxhall, Warwickshire. She died in 1680 and their only child, a son, William, died two years later. Richard then married Anne, daughter of Sir Francis Russell of Strensham. In 1684 he became sheriff of Worcestershire, an office he held until his death three years later. His widow remarried twice, but herself survived until 1735. She was renowned for her strong attachment to her own money, and refusal to surrender control of funds to any of her husbands, a trait which brought her into conflict with the new owner of Madresfield when she disputed her liability to pay for a horseman in the Militia. For on Richard's death Madresfield passed into the care of the colonel's second son, William, and began at last the revival of its fortunes under the stabilising influence of an astute owner.

CHAPTER THREE
William the Correspondent

William Lygon (1642-1721) is known as 'the Correspondent' in order to distinguish him from the two Williams who preceded him and the two who followed him. The designation originated from his collection of 800 letters, which supply us with the first detailed picture of a member of the family at Madresfield Court.

William was born in September, 1642, the year of Charles 1's disastrous attempt at Nottingham to rally the provinces against his Parliamentary opponents in London. His childhood was lived in the shadow of civil war and of a father who, however reluctantly, had taken up arms against his king. The first sign of impending conflict had been the issue, in August, 1642, of writs instructing parish constables to summon an assembly of bands of armed and trained men at Pitchcroft, now the site of Worcester's racecourse. Shortly after William's birth the first battle of the war was fought at Powick Bridge on 23 September. A see-saw existence followed, with Royalist and Parliamentary forces alternating in control. Worcestershire especially suffered throughout the troubled years; the county was frequently subjected to the billeting of soldiers—at one time over 12,000 around Upton-upon-Severn alone—and consequent recurrent demands on the local community for supplies for both men and horses.

As a second son, young William could not expect a prolonged formal education at university, but he fared better than many of his contemporaries. When his father died in 1681, he left 530 books and 11 maps, as well as 43 pictures, which suggests a man of some culture for his time. Equally significant is the fact that the quantity of silver in the house had more than doubled in the period between the death of William the Wasteful and the Colonel's, although the long list of mortgaged properties remained substantially the same. Perhaps confinement for over 20 years to Madresfield had robbed the Colonel of interest in properties which, although he still owned, he could not visit. William's own correspondence also indicates at least an acquaintance with classical literature and a knowledge of Greek, as well as particular interest in theology and mathematics.

It may have been his keen interest in mathematics rather than the law (three of his brothers became barristers) which led to his being apprenticed at the age of 15 to Richard Izard, a member of the Grocers' Livery Company in London. The arrangement must have been a relief to the Colonel for he finally had six sons and four daughters to support. Although Samuel Knightley had died, through that connection young William could count on a number of influential friends in the City. His aunt, Margaret, was living in Westminster, and he was joined the following year by his younger brother Thomas, who was apprenticed to another grocer, Francis Lucy.

The choice of the Grocers' Livery Company was shrewd. It is said to have been incorporated in 1344, and is second only to the Mercers' in precedence. The Livery Companies—there are now over 80, including Scientific Instrument Makers and Airline Pilots—had their origin in the guilds of craftsmen in the Middle Ages and were formed for the protection of their trading interests. Admission was usually by apprenticeship to a craftsman member. The Grocers were originally merchants dealing in commodities sold by the 'gross', especially foodstuffs such as spices, tea, and dried fruits. Often very wealthy, they exercised great influence both in their own sphere and more widely; on numerous occasions they had supplied London with its Lord Mayor. The powers of these companies have in some instances continued to the present day, for example the Goldsmiths' 'hallmarking' of precious metals and the Gunsmiths' 'proofing' small arms. In the case of the Grocers, their weekly meeting to determine the market price of tea was discontinued only in 1998. Most of the companies are governed by self-appointed bodies known as 'courts of assistants', presided over by a prime and other wardens, a system which was to cause William Lygon so much argument in later life.

In 1657 trade was rapidly expanding. Improved shipping and new markets in recently discovered countries meant that new imports had their counterpart in fresh opportunities for exports. Tea, chocolate and coffee, and a great variety of spices from the East, were beginning to reach the more affluent households in England. The opportunities for advancement, without necessarily risking one's life as military service entailed, must have attracted many ambitious young men who were willing to take risks of another nature. The ships docking at London brought news of strange lands overseas and it began to be possible to travel in pursuit no longer of elusive gold, but rather for calico or turkeys or potatoes or tobacco—and to make good money out of the travelling. Perhaps young William also remembered his father's 11 maps, and began to understand their purpose, though if they followed the map making traditions of the 14th and 15th centuries they would have shown an enlarged British Isles, Jerusalem at the centre and coastlines that bore little resemblance to reality.

But his career had a chequered beginning. In his own words, on leaving home his father had given him 'a poor £600', the most he could eventually have expected to receive as his share of the estate, and on this 'he made shift to live like a gentleman', but he lost most of his capital in the Great Fire of London in September, 1666. In March, 1667, aged 24, and having completed his apprenticeship in about 1664, he was admitted as a Freeman of the Grocers' Livery Company. Four years later he entered into partnership with another grocer, Thomas Tuckfield of Broad Street. At some stage he married a young woman of whom nothing is known, except that she was named Elizabeth Bridges and that she died young and childless. For many years William did not remarry.

William was an astute businessman, but he had also a keen interest in politics, and like many of his contemporaries he spent much of his time in the new coffee houses in London. In that sophisticated life, where the latest scandal at Court vied with the day's market news as the main topic, the countrified life of Madresfield must have seemed a million miles away. Even the coach journey between city and home took between two and four days. His mother died, and then his father in 1681; his brother Richard inherited, as expected. Richard was already a widower, and his only son died in 1682. He remarried within a few months, but had no further children, and therefore when he died in April, 1687, William found himself in possession of Madresfield and its estates.

So William's quietly successful career as a London merchant was abruptly terminated. He had to leave the bustle and excitement of London and return to Worcestershire to try to remedy the failing fortunes of Lygon, for with the troubled times of the Civil War and his father's enforced restriction to Madresfield following the extravagances of his great-grandfather, the Lygon finances were at a very low ebb. The estate was further impoverished by annuities left to his sisters, and also by the claim of his brother's widow to a considerable share. As he wrote in 1706, when protesting against his nomination by the Grocers' Company as Sheriff of London for the coming year: 'I'm all that is left of my family and upon the death of my brother, by which that little of the Estate that is left fell to me, I resolved to live as handsomely upon it as my circumstances would bear, which I have accordingly done and suppose *that* the occasion [of] my having and giving you this trouble. It's the misfortune of a family sometimes that their predecessors have had an estate, especially where the reputation shall be kept up tho' three quarters of it be sold away. I suppose mine is thus represented to my Lord Mayor, which makes me thus taken notice of. Sir, the favour I beg if you have any acquaintance with the present Lord Mayor [is] that you would be pleased to let him know by two lines that he is misinformed of my estate in thinking me fit for such an office, and to desire him to pass me by without taking any notice of me.' His plea was accepted on this occasion, fortunately, for otherwise he would have been fined £400; on a previous occasion he had had to pay £20 to avoid nomination. Because of numerous similar appeals the system was later amended.

He returned to his childhood home after 30 years' absence, a widower with no children. As he saw it, his immediate task was to find a suitable wife, for he was 45 and he wanted an heir. Within a year he had decided on Margaret, only child and heiress of Thomas Corbyn of Hall End near Polesworth in Warwickshire. William may already have been acquainted with the Corbyns, for members of that family were traders with the West Indies. Thomas Corbyn was in failing health; he came to live at Madresfield after the wedding in 1688, but died within a few months. Unfortunately he had made no written will, and although his 'noncupative' will (made verbally in the presence of witnesses) was declared perfectly valid, William found himself at variance for several years with the male members of the Corbyn family, who had expected to inherit much that instead went to the newcomer who had so recently married their cousin.

But it was a happy marriage. Margaret, like the majority of women of her time, had had little if any education and was almost illiterate, but the only comment William ever recorded about her was made after her death and hinted at his affection for her: 'My dear wife had brought up her eldest boy so tenderly that I feared that he would be spoiled, and when I told her of it had nothing but tears in answer, [so] that had she lived much longer it would have been hard to have reared him and made anything of him.' Since he himself was very far from being a harsh disciplinarian, his wife must indeed have been indulgent.

Much of his time after his return to Madresfield was at first spent in learning about agriculture, and struggling to sort out the financial difficulties, but his letters—the only source of information—do not give much information about the details; his correspondence has other purposes. There is the management of his capital and of his slowly increasing investments, for which he relied greatly on the advice of Thomas Tuckfield, his ex-trading partner; and then his abiding interest in politics.

He remained for the rest of his life in contact with local Members of Parliament who kept him well-informed about Westminster happenings, and who were also eager to secure his influence at every election. William was not always ready to declare his support, and since the party system was not yet fully developed he was free on each occasion to choose where to bestow his favour. His friends were often members of opposing factions, and he took care not to enter into any long-term allegiances. At the time, of course, landowners had considerable influence, not to say control, over the votes of their tenants and freeholders; as one candidate wrote anxiously in 1702, when he heard that his rival was giving a 'treat'—i.e. a substantial meal to any who might support him: '… it were well if there were caution given to the freeholders to prevent their going to it that they may not be drawn into any engagement. When the freeholders begin to sell their votes for beef and ale they themselves may be sold in good time.'

The same pattern of discretion is repeated in every election where Lygon's support was canvassed, for it was seldom readily apparent. He seems to have been influenced perhaps more by personal friendships than by political opinions, and considerable independence of thought. He had on many points quite strong opinions, though on the whole he rejected any embryonic party label, and perhaps he should be judged by his clearest pronouncement on the subject of labels in general, made when years later he was recalling the negotiations for the marriage of Lord Digby's daughter with his eldest son. She had objected on the grounds that the father of her proposed bridegroom was a Whig and a Low Churchman, and Lygon responded in his forthright fashion that if constant attendance at the Church and the Sacrament was the character of a Low Churchman, 'then I must confess myself of that party. As for State affairs, it had always been my principle to have the prerogatives and privileges keep their bounds, and I would be as unwilling to have the privileges of the people gain upon the prerogatives of the prince, as to have the prerogatives of the prince invade the people's privileges. If this be Whiggism then I must own myself one of them.'

William fortunately displayed the same moderation in another matter where less cautious men were persuaded towards disaster. At the beginning of 1720 the South Sea Company's scheme known to history as the 'South Sea Bubble' gained notice, and a fever of speculation spread rapidly through all classes. It seemed incredible that, as one of his friends wrote, 'what cost but 97$^{1}/_{2}$ became worth 120 within a few days'. Lygon invested a small amount, but sold before the crash, possibly due to Roger Tuckfield, who had consistently shown marked distrust of the scheme and whose judgement was vindicated before the end of the year.

His family life also demanded considerable strength of character. His wife Margaret died in 1699, only 11 years after their marriage, and left Lygon with four young children. His eldest son, another William, was sent, as befitted the heir to Madresfield, to Balliol College. After he had completed his time at Oxford, Lygon's urgent concern was to find him a suitable wife. The custom of the time was still for a marriage to be formally arranged by negotiation between the respective parents, though the final decision was often left to the young couple. Although William's prospects as the future owner of the now more prosperous Madresfield estates were a considerable asset, Lygon had considerable difficulty in finding a bride for his son, especially since he insisted that there must be genuine affection between the parties. At least some six possibilities were explored without success. This somewhat delayed matters; however, at last a suitable match was arranged with Margaret, daughter of Charles Cocks of Worcester, a member of a long-established family of lawyers. The young couple were married on 2 August, 1716, when the bridegroom was aged 25. On 4 September he died from an unspecified fever. His young widow lived on at Madresfield for some months, and though she later remarried, to the future first Earl of Hardwicke, she remained on very close terms with her first father-in-law, to whom she wrote as 'your affectionate Friend'.

In 1711 his third son, Thomas, had died at the age of 15 from smallpox contracted whilst at school in Worcester. So now Lygon had to find a bride for his only remaining son, Corbyn. However, Corbyn was quite severely handicapped, and Lygon had had considerable difficulty in finding a suitable master for him when he opted to become a grocer. But Corbyn had barely completed his apprenticeship in 1716 when his elder brother died, and he was immediately summoned to return to Madresfield as the heir. It was the custom that as the owner of Madresfield advanced in years, his heir became his understudy, gradually taking an increasing share in the administration of the estates.

Lygon was now 64, a good age for those days, and particularly for the male members of the Lygon family. He had rescued the estates' finances from their nadir, though he was still having arguments with the Grocers' Livery Company about their continual demands. Because of his length of service, and even more because of his reputed wealth, although he had left London and had ceased to operate as a merchant, he was nominated as the Company's Warden in 1697 and had to pay a fine for refusing the appointment. In 1706 and 1714 he was nominated against his wishes as Sheriff of London and Middlesex, and experienced great opposition in being excused from the appointment.

Despite the rumours of his alleged wealth, rather than of his predecessors' financial difficulties, Lygon experienced some difficulty in finding a wife for Corbyn, but the situation looked promising when the daughter of Edmund Bray of Barrington Park in Gloucestershire was suggested by Anthony Lechmere, a member of a long-established Worcestershire family. Lechmere conducted the negotiations and her parents were enthusiastic; however, the 'Simple Chit', as one correspondent called her, proved to have a mind of her own, and, as her father wrote, the caprice of a girl put an end to an affair from which he had expected the greatest satisfaction. But then events took an unexpected turn. Corbyn's old master, Isaac Waldo, negotiated a match with Jane, daughter of Isaac Tullie, who was a London silk mercer. He was also a brother-in-law of Edmund Bray, and there was some concern in case Miss Tullie might be adversely influenced by her cousin Miss Bray. These fears proved to be unfounded, and Corbyn and Jane were married only two months later, in 1717. Perhaps Jane Tullie understood Corbyn's struggle with his physical difficulties, for she herself was 'very much marked by smallpox'.

William showed a great deal of concern for the future of the estates. During his life at Madresfield he revoked no fewer than seven wills, and it was the eighth which eventually gained probate. It has to be borne in mind that the deaths of his sons and his wife, as well as difficulties with his son-in-law (see p.21), again and again upset his plans. There is one interesting bequest that led to a little trouble in the next century, when the ratepayers of Madresfield endeavoured, not unusually, to avoid a liability properly theirs. He left 'To the parishioners of Madresfield £12 to build three bridges of stone or brick one in the lane as you go from Matchfield Green to the Mill, one other a little below the Mill over the brook, and the third in Millfield above the Pitt at the upper end of my eighteen acres.' The parishioners stoutly refused to accept any liability for repairing the bridges on the grounds that they had been built primarily to protect the privacy of the landowner, which was incontrovertible, and as by then the Lygons had inherited considerable wealth, the matter was allowed to drop.

Modern visitors will know these bridges over the 'Back Drive'; there was a blacksmith's forge close to where North Lodge now stands, and beyond that an old water mill, (on whose site the Victorian 'Rock Garden' was constructed). All that remains today of 'Matchfield Green' is the minute triangle of grass near the black and white house known as 'Byeways' next to Hayswood Farm. In its day it was a sizeable piece of land, though not so large perhaps as Madresfield's other public space, 'Boon's Green', at the junction of Pinner's (now Rectory) Lane with North End Lane.

CHAPTER FOUR
Waiting for a New Dawn

After the death of William Lygon in 1721, Madresfield settled down to a quiet, untroubled existence which lasted for the greater part of the 18th century.

Corbyn Lygon, (1694-1728), being a second son, like his father had no expectation of a prolonged education or of inheriting the estates. But in addition he had two physical handicaps with which he battled all his life. He was extremely lame, partly due to having been born with a club foot, and he is recorded as having an impediment in his speech which was probably excessive stammering. As mentioned, William Lygon considered his wife to have been far too indulgent with their first son, and one suspects that even the father abandoned any ideas of discipline when he had to deal with Corbyn's difficulties. There are repeated references to his search for a cure. For instance, in November, 1701 when Corbyn was seven years old, William wrote to Mr. Mountjoy, a 'sopeboyler' in Bristol: 'Good Sir, My Cosin Whittingham tells me you … would come hither to perfect the cure of my son, whereby to bring his leggs strait, which he gives me hope you can affect [*sic*]… I will continue the use of the ointment according to directions.'

When Corbyn was 15 years old, serious consideration was given to his future career, if any proved possible. Following his own experience, his father sent him to stay with his old friends the Tuckfields in London to make a choice of whatever business appealed to him. After two months of consideration, Corbyn opted to become a grocer as his father had been.

His friends were dubious. A grocer's apprentice could still expect to have to carry out the more unpleasant tasks such as sweeping the floors, running errands and delivering verbal messages. However, he was adamant in his choice. At last a suitable master was found who already employed a manservant to do the menial tasks and who, because of his regard for William Lygon as a senior member of the Grocers Livery Company, was willing to give Corbyn a trial. So the boy was formally apprenticed to Isaac Waldo, and fortunately he proved to be both very willing and extremely capable despite his handicaps. His lameness persisted, in spite of treatment over many years which seems to have consisted mainly of the application of various ointments. In addition, he had several sessions of what would now be called speech therapy with a practitioner in Kensington, although the benefit of these treatments seems never to have been long-lived.

Corbyn sent his father meticulous accounts of his expenses. He was especially careful of his personal appearance, perhaps in an attempt to compensate for his disabilities. When he was first apprenticed, he celebrated by acquiring a new coat, six handkerchiefs and a velvet cap; later he reports having bought from a Mercer a fustian frock and breeches 'to be a little handsome when I go out with Bills'. More importantly, he seems to have been generally well-liked and respected, and his master spoke well of him.

But Corbyn had hardly completed his apprenticeship in 1716 when his elder brother died and he was immediately summoned back to Madresfield to take his place as the heir. There ensued the negotiations, mentioned above, for a suitable bride, and the humiliation of being found unsuitable, which may well have been the result of the discussions with Mr. Bray. But Miss Tullie and Corbyn were married on 4 June, 1717, only two months after their marriage was first discussed, and came to live at Madresfield. Their son was born in May, 1720, to the unbounded delight of Isaac Tullie, who wrote promising to set off as soon as possible for Worcestershire 'to make our glorious boy a Christian', and to bring with him a Christening present of £100, sending in advance a keg of sturgeon. The infant was, of course, named William.

As well as his son, Corbyn had two daughters, Jane and Margaret, though his marriage, like his father's, was ended by death within 11 years. His wife died in May, 1728, and his own death followed a few months later. One daughter, Jane, had already died, and he was survived by his young son William who died in 1730 and his daughter Margaret who died unmarried in 1741. Corbyn had control of the estates for only seven years. There are practically no records of his ownership now extant, but one gains the impression of a courageous young man who struggled with considerable success against adversity.

In 1713 Corbyn's sister, Margaret, the eldest child of William the Correspondent, had married Reginald, son of Thomas Pyndar of Kempley in Gloucestershire. It was a marriage which was to bring into Lygon ownership several important estates in Derbyshire and various properties in Gloucestershire.

The Pindars—who spelt their surname Pyndar, Pindar or Pynder depending on which branch of the family was their origin or from whom they had benefited by inheritance—had acquired considerable wealth and importance through their descent from Sir Paul Pindar who, born in 1566 the son of Thomas Pindar a merchant in Wellingborough, had spent a number of years abroad first as a trader in Venice and later as ambassador for James I at Constantinople. On his permanent return to England in 1623 he is said to have brought with him a great fortune in jewels, and he subsequently became a very successful financier. In 1636 his fortune was valued at £236,000, an almost incredible sum for that period, though by the time of his death in 1650 it had decreased considerably. He left a third of his property to the children of his nephew, also Paul Pyndar (which seems to have been the spelling adopted by the Herefordshire branch of the family). However, this Paul left only one surviving child, Mary, who inherited all her great-uncle Sir Paul's legacy, and it is through her that the Pindar estates in Herefordshire, and also, through purchase, in Derbyshire, eventually came into the possession of her nearest surviving relative, her great-nephew the Reginald Pyndar who married Margaret Lygon in 1713. When, in 1813,

John Reginald Lygon, son of the first Earl Beauchamp, succeeded in his claim to the Pindar Lincolnshire estates as the nearest living descendant of Mary Pindar, he adopted for his new surname the spelling 'Pindar'.

After the marriage, Reginald came to live with Margaret at Madresfield Court for a brief period, but his stay came to an abrupt end when William expelled him on the grounds of despicable behaviour. Although the reason is not explicitly recorded, the explanation may lie in the fact that whilst the date of the marriage appears in ecclesiastical records as 25 June, 1713, there is no corresponding record of her son's birth date. However, when eventually—in order to inherit Madresfield—he had to change his surname on his coming of age, his birth date appears as 24 May, 1712. If in fact he was illegitimate, this may have been the reason for William Lygon's antipathy, for he was a man of deep religious convictions and firmly held principles. There are also indications that Margaret, his first child and only daughter, held a special place in his affections. Reginald's mother pleaded for his reinstatement on the grounds of his ill-health (possibly alcoholism), but, hardly surprisingly in view of his own son Corbyn's brave battle against difficulties, William proved sceptical, and although the matter was to some extent smoothed over, it is evident from his later actions that he continued to have no confidence in the young man.

Margaret and Reginald then went to live at Hallow Park, near Worcester, the former home of her aunt Anne Bull (sister of the Correspondent) where they appear to have lived for most of the eight years until Reginald's death. Anne's husband was a member of a very influential family and this was a connection that proved as helpful to the Lygons as her mother's marriage to Samuel Knightley had been in the previous generation. Anne, whose only child had died young and whose husband predeceased her, left her property at Hallow Park in trust for Corbyn's only surviving daughter Margaret; Reginald Pyndar was one of the trustees and there was at one time a suggestion that he had defrauded her, though this allegation was never investigated. This Margaret Lygon died in 1741, when she was just 20; she had been living near the sea at Bristol for health reasons. Margaret and Reginald Pyndar also spent several periods at The Stone House in Kempley, which was a Pyndar property. They had three sons, Reginald, Philip and William; the two younger sons both became merchants in London.

Because of his unease about Reginald's character, and also the probability that Corbyn might not live to old age, William Lygon had crafted his will carefully to ensure that his unsatisfactory son-in-law's control so far as the Madresfield estates were concerned, should be curtailed. In the event, Reginald died only a few months after William Lygon in 1721.

Margaret returned to Madresfield after her brother's death in 1728 with her three sons. Her return was shortly followed by the death of Corbyn's son, William, in 1730, so Margaret stayed on until her eldest son attained his majority in 1733. Within a few days of the formalities being completed, by which he took possession of the estates, his mother left to marry Francis Biddulph of Ledbury. She had a son the following year, and died shortly after his birth.

Reginald Pyndar, in accordance with the conditions laid down in his grandfather's will, assumed by Act of Parliament in 1733 the name and arms of Lygon in lieu of those of Pyndar. In 1739 he married Susanna Hanmer, daughter of William Hanmer of Bettesfield in Flintshire and first cousin of William Jennens, a member of an extremely wealthy family of ironmasters in Birmingham. But he seems not to have resided permanently at Madresfield Court, preferring Hallow Park, and there is little evidence of any lasting effect on the Lygon estates. An entry in the Supplement to Nash's *History of Worcestershire* gives a clear indication of his character, although it is probably somewhat franker in some respects than would appear in a modern obituary. It was written by a former tutor, the Rev. James Gyles:

> In the *Worcester Journal* dated 1 January, 1789, appeared the following paragraphs, written by Rev. Mr. Gyles of Powick, formerly tutor to William Lygon, son to Reginald Lygon esquire:
> 'On Christmas Day died suddenly at his seat at Hallow Park in this county, Reginald Lygon, the sole mention of whose name will immediately bring to the recollection of his acquaintance the idea of all the useful and amiable virtues that can adorn and dignify the character of a good man. His life, which was long, happy and honourable was spent in constant, unwearied and unremitted exertions in the service of his country, his friends and his neighbours. As a magistrate, in which capacity he acted more than 50 years, during which time he hardly ever missed an Assize or Quarter Sessions, (viz. one hundred Assizes, two hundred Quarter Sessions; at a very great number of the latter he was Chairman), he was a conscientious supporter of the laws, to which he gave vigour and efficacy, by precipt [*sic*], by affability, liberal hospitality, and general philanthropy; and by a peculiar delicacy of manners he won the hearts and secured the respect of all who had the happiness of knowing him.
> The loss of a man so useful, so responsible, so revered and so beloved, will be long felt and deeply regretted: but alas when shall it be repaired?'
> What is here said of Mr Lygon is strictly true; but he had one merit unknown to those who were not intimate with him, and in which he excelled even Socrates, or any of the ancient philosophers; he was naturally of a very hasty, peevish and passionate temper, which, by his strict attention to the principles and practice of the Christian religion, particularly as to the government of his mind, he entirely conquered and scarcely ever lost himself, and in the course of his life he was remarkable for meekness and moderation as for any other virtue whatsoever.
> He went to church on Xmas Day, the weather being very severe, received the Sacrament, and returned home seemingly in perfect health; eat [*sic*] an hearty dinner at three o'clock, about four was seized with a vomiting, took a gentle emetic and some tea, and died in his parlour about six; probably it was owing to the gout in his stomach; and had he taken a warm cordial perhaps this valuable life would have been preserved for some years.

There is still in the Court library an interesting reminder of the Pindar connection—a small group of volumes known as 'the Pindar Collection'. These are mostly 17th-century legal tomes, but their outstanding feature is several manuscripts bound in one volume by

> **THE PROVISIONS** of five tonnes of Gascony wyne and the charges of the same whiche wyne is layed into the Starchamber Seller at Westmʳ for the s'vice of the 11s and other of her maᵗⁱᵉˢ most honorable privye Counsell for the XLIIᵗʰ yeere of her highness most happye Raigne.
>
> Imprimis payed to Mʳ Ald'man Lee for 5 Tonnes of Gascoigne wyne after the rate of xviijˡⁱ the tonne (whereof deducted viijˡⁱ xvjˢ for the new Impost) xxiiijˡⁱ iiijˢ Item for the cariage of the same wyne from London to the Starchamber Seller xijˢ Item payed to the porters for loading unloading & Cowching the said wyne into the seller xijˢ Item to the Cowp's for their helpe in tasting & choicing the said wynes & in looking to them xiijˢ iiijᵈ Item for the Stewardes boothire to & from Westᵐ div's tymes goeing about the said wynes vˢ Item to the Cowp' for vjᶜ newe hoopes & chynes sett on the hh' of the said wynes xlˢ Item for his boothire iiijˢ Item for the Cowp's dynn's at Westᵐ at the hooping of the said wynes vijˢ Item ij ells of canvas to stoppe the bunghooles ijˢ viijᵈ Item for xx gallons of Clarrett wyne to fill up the hh. that leaked by the way xlˢ Item for ij loades of gravell to laye in the seller ijˢ in all
>
> xxᵢᵢᵢⱼᵥⱼˡⁱxjˢ
>
> Ex' Sum' p' Alexʳ King Audit'
>
>   Tho. Egerton   T. Buchurst
>
> Toˡⁱˢ 259ˡⁱ-10ˢ-8ᵈ   88ˡⁱ-11-0ᵈ

A transcript of one of the accounts held at Madresfield Court for provisioning the Star Chamber with wine. Note the item for topping up the quantity as a result of leakage

the seventh earl under the title of 'The Dyette of the Star Chamber'. These are accounts for the years 1595, 1599 and 1603. At that time, Matthew Pindar, brother of the famous Sir Paul mentioned above, was a Clerk to Chancery, and this possibly explains their eventual transfer to Madresfield. It is understood that for these particular three years, no accounts are held in the Public Record Office.

The Court of the Star Chamber (so named because the room in which it met had a ceiling decorated with stars) was set up in 1516, and should not be confused with the short-lived tribunal of the same name in 1487. It initially earned great respect for its fairness, in particular in guarding the interests of the yeomanry as against the nobility. There is no evidence that it ever employed torture in its investigations. It was through the Court of the Star Chamber, the real governing body of Tudor England, that the power of the Crown was exerted. By 1547 it consisted of privy councillors, assisted by judges, and was largely used for civil cases which involved violence, as it adopted a simple system and worked in English. Over a long period it fell into disrepute, eventually being seen as a threat to liberties rather than upholding them. The Court sat regularly during the legal terms of Hilary, Easter, Trinity and Michaelmas and attendance at the dinners it held each term almost became part of the requirement for would-be barristers, and many peers also attended. It is said that the average number present at these dinners was about 40, one of the most regular attenders being Bishop Whitgift (1530-1604) of Worcester, later Archbishop of Canterbury. Although often called 'Whitebait' or 'Fish' dinners—sometimes as many as 30 varieties of fish were served—the menu usually included meat as well, even during Lent. No doubt the meals provided an informal opportunity for discussion of important matters, perhaps a faint forerunner of the retirement of a modern jury to consider its verdict.

The title of the manuscripts held at Madresfield is somewhat misleading. They do not deal with the proceedings of the Court as such, but with the catering and what are perhaps best described as general housekeeping expenses such as payment of domestic staff, purchase and transport of various items (as when James I on his accession authorised the laying down of a new cellar of vintage wines), some building repairs and purchase of furniture, and in great detail the amounts and cost of every item of food supplied and consumed.

The Court's reputation was severely affected by official manipulation in the reigns of James I and Charles I, and it was finally abolished in 1641, but the system of having a panel of special advisors to the monarch continued and survives in the form of The Privy Council, and as members of that body almost three centuries later the sixth and seventh Earls Beauchamp pledged their loyalty and secrecy in the same oath. Its wording is unambiguous in its demands; with his hand on the Bible the would-be councillor was instructed:

> You shall swear to be a true and faithful Servant unto the King's Majesty, as one of His Majesty's Privy Council. You shall not know or understand of any manner of thing to be attempted, done, or spoken against His Majesty's Person, Honour, Crown, or Dignity Royal; but you shall lett and withstand ['lett' means 'oppose' as in the phrase 'without let or hindrance'] the same to the uttermost of your Power, and either cause it to be revealed to His Majesty Himself, or to such of His Privy Council as shall advertise His Majesty of the same. You shall, in all things to be moved, treated, and debated in Council, faithfully and truly declare your Mind and Opinion, according to your Heart and Conscience; and shall keep secret all matters committed and revealed unto you, or that shall be treated of secretly in Council. And if any of the said Treaties or Councils shall touch any of the Counsellors, you shall not reveal it unto him, but shall keep the same until such time as, by the consent of His Majesty, or of the Council, Publication shall be made thereof. You shall to your uttermost bear faith and allegiance unto the King's Majesty; and shall assist and defend all Jurisdictions, Pre-eminences, and Authorities, granted to His Majesty, and annexed to the Crown by Acts of Parliament, or otherwise, against all Foreign Princes, Persons, Prelates, States, or Potentates. And generally in all things you shall do as a faithful and true Servant ought to do to His Majesty.
>
> So help you God, and the Holy Contents of this Book.

CHAPTER FIVE
William Lygon, First Earl Beauchamp (1747-1816)

William Lygon, only son of Reginald (Pyndar) Lygon, was born in 1747 and was educated privately at home, matriculating at Oxford in 1764. Little is known about his early life, but at some stage he became acquainted with William Pitt the Elder and later became a close friend of Pitt the Younger. Lygon entered Parliament as the Member for Worcestershire in 1806, and in due course was appointed to the Board (later the Ministry) of Agriculture. A quiet, studious man, he must have seemed to many the epitome of caution and modesty, not a man to set the Thames on fire, and likely to retire in due course to live in obscurity on his country estates. But in 1780 he married, and in 1798 inherited a fortune, two events which changed radically the life of the Lygons of Madresfield.

It is probably significant that there are no records of any negotiations regarding his marriage—a fact extraordinary in itself, since the marriage of the heir to Madresfield had always been most carefully arranged. Perhaps his father, born a Pyndar and knowing how his own father had been mistrusted, and possibly feeling alienated from Madresfield—for he spent little time at the Court—felt unwilling to follow the tradition of finding a suitable bride for his son. There is room for much speculation, but there is no certainty why William Lygon was allowed to choose a bride named Catherine Denne, whose ancestry was not well known except that her mother was the daughter of a gentleman in Somerset and a friend of a well-known society hostess, Mrs. Margaret Manisty of Richmond, mother of a prominent judge.

But there is one clue which only serves to whet our curiosity. James Denne used as his personal seal the arms of the Dennes of Grenane in Co. Kilkenny. This was a long-established family of landowners, whose great offence in the eyes of their English rulers had been to refuse to abandon their Catholic faith. They had been obdurate recusants, well-known for their sheltering of priests. To put this in perspective, it must be remembered that in their endeavour to stamp out Roman Catholicism in Ireland, the authorities had used a carrot and stick approach. The carrot was the reward of £5 for the betrayal of any priest's hiding place. This amount was probably considered appropriate as it equated to the reward one could earn for bringing in the head of a dead wolf, also the object of extermination, and which had a biblical connotation that was irresistible to the current authorities. The stick was the sequestration of all lands belonging to the priest's protector. In the event of a family's property, any member, regardless of seniority, by attending just one Protestant service in a year, could gain possession of the inheritance.

In the 17th century, all the Denne lands were sequestrated, and of the family of 12 children to which James Denne's grandfather probably belonged, none would compromise. Instead, he fled to Bristol. James evidently still prided himself on his descent, signified by the old seal preserved at Madresfield. It is interesting that the mother of William Pitt the Elder came from Co. Waterford, adjacent to Co. Kilkenny; she was a member of the Villiers family and one wonders if the family benefitted from the sequestration of the Denne lands. Such a suggestion may seem far-fetched to a modern reader, but H.V. Morton, an English writer of the 1930s has a valuable insight in his book *In Search of Ireland*:

'There is not a great estate in Ireland owned by one of Cromwell's settlers which had not always had a ghostly other owner in the memory of the common people. He may be only a legend or he may be somebody "up in the hills"; but he is not forgotten. It all proves that in Ireland there is no ancient history: all history is contemporary.'

Catherine Denne, Countess Beauchamp by John Hoppner RA

Whatever her origins, Catherine Denne was attractive and vivacious, and a good organiser. She settled down as William Lygon's wife and dutifully produced and reared four sons and six daughters, and Madresfield Court came to life again. She also managed to keep in touch with London life, as the couple had a house in Great George Street in Westminster and subsequently bought one in St. James' Square. As an MP he was often in London. Then 1798 dawned.

It was an unlikely year for an Irishwoman to succeed in London society, for the Irish were rebelling again, this time with greater success than usual. But on 19 June William Jennens, ancestor of William's mother Susanna Hanmer, died within a few weeks of his 98th birthday. He had made no will, and so his estate was divided between his three nearest kinsfolk. It has been computed that William Lygon's share amounted to approximately £80 million in 1999 terms. Jennens' estate took many forms of property: buildings, mortgages—the list of borrowers, kept in a tiny notebook, whose loans were still outstanding, reads like a condensed Debrett's—silver, glass, pictures and much besides. After several visits to his house at Richmond, the lawyers even located and accounted for some £23,000 in cash. Whilst Jennens had inherited much of his fortune from several bachelor uncles, some of his wealth was attributed to his extreme thrift—he would light a candle if a visitor came to discuss business, but considered darkness sufficient for social chit-chat. He was descended from two or three generations of ironmasters in Birmingham who had been so successful that despite the lack of distinguished forbears he had been blessed with two important godparents—William III and Mary. A relative was Charles Jennens (1700-1773), Handel's librettist for 'Messiah'. Although, because of the immense sums involved, there were inevitably a number of lawsuits brought by hopeful claimants over a long period, none of these was successful. The Jennens modern millions were equally divided between three claimants—William Lygon, Mary Viscountess Andover and George Augustus Curzon.

William Lygon sorted out financial matters slowly and methodically in his usual meticulous style. There is an interesting entry noting the particulars of someone's repayment of a debt of £3,000; Lygon noted an overcharge of 1s. 9d. (about 8p) and promptly refunded it. His letters clearly reflect his interests and his character, dealing with purchases of properties, settlements on his children to whom he was devoted, and often kind responses to begging letters.

Before 1798 the Lygons had been on the fringe of London society. Now they were welcomed eagerly. Typical is a letter in 1803 from the Duchess of Sussex, wife of the Prince of Wales's brother, who wrote:

> The Duchess of Sussex sends her Compliments to Mr. Lygon [and hopes] he will pardon the liberty she takes (not having the advantage of either His or Mrs. Lygon's acquaintance) if she requests him to have the goodness to call upon her, any hour most convenient for Mr. Lygon will equally accommodate the Duchess, if he will only let her know it, so that she may take care to be at home.

Perhaps the Duchess needed a loan.

Catherine Denne, Countess Beauchamp by Sir Joshua Reynolds

For William's wife Catherine the advent of wealth was immensely liberating. Hitherto she had been the dutiful wife, devoted mother and capable housekeeper. Now she added a new role to her repertoire. It is not clear when exactly she opened her campaign to secure a title, but it cannot have been long delayed after the Jennens inheritance. Gossip at the time invariably credited Catherine rather than her husband with the ambition, but perhaps it was mutual. A letter from her great-granddaughter, Lady Mary Lygon, in 1892, written to her brother the seventh earl from a country house she was visiting, shines some light on this question. She had been reading a collection of her host's collection of historic letters: 'There were also 3 volumes of applications and requests made to Mr Pitt while he was in office, for preferments, peerages, offices, money and every sort of thing. I discovered 3 from "Mr Lyggon" asking for a Peerage!'

But more enlightening is the following letter from Francis Townsend, Windsor Herald at the time of the advancement of the Barony to an Earldom in 1816:

> My dear Lord, ...
> When Your Lordship says you don't believe that ten years ago [i.e. at the granting of the Barony] you would have given any Woman credit for so much perseverance and success, I think you forgot, for the moment, that I have been near thrice ten years acquainted with the Countess. I will admit that I don't now know any other Woman to whom I could give that Credit; But I have repeatedly said, that in the whole course of my professional Life (of more than 44 years duration) I never met with any one, male or female, who could more clearly explain, or more dextrously secure, (I had almost said seduce,) Attention to the Business in hand in which she took an interest. - Permit me the pleasure of adding, that no one can more sincerely rejoice in her success than I do ...

Quoting the gossips again, it was said that Catherine had paid £800 for the title 'Baron Beauchamp of Powyke', gazetted in December, 1806; a decade later and only a year before her husband's death when it was advanced to an Earldom, again it was Catherine who was reported to have paid £10,000 to the Exchequer. Some persuasion was undoubtedly required to secure the revival of the Beauchamp title, since William's claim to this was only through the female line some four centuries earlier. It was not then considered so reprehensible to 'encourage' the Crown's favour, but the attribution to the wife's persistence is significant. It is also significant that during the lawsuit over the Jennens estate—so protracted that it is said to have inspired Dickens with the tragedy of the Jarndyce v. Jarndyce suit in *Bleak House*—the Heralds' Office who had been closely involved with tracing the genealogy of the many Jennens claimants, wrote to Catherine, not to her husband, reassuringly and deferentially, that she need fear nothing from the claim made by 'your Hibernian cousin'. Nothing is now known about this matter, though it reinforces Catherine's Irish background.

Pitt had also to find an opportune time to recommend Lygon's ennoblement and it came when there was a reshuffle of Admiralty appointments. One of Pitt's nominees, Sir Charles Middleton, was being made a Baron, and it was believed at the time that Sir Benjamin Blomfield, private secretary to George III, seized the opportunity to advance

Lygon without incurring accusations of favouritism. The initiative was made to appear as the king's in the letter which Blomfield wrote on 22 April, 1805: 'The King thinks that it would be advisable, on this addition [i.e. Middleton's] to the Peerage, to advance Mr. Lygon, the Member for The County of Worcester, whose excellent character, steady support of Government, and very large fortune, place him in a situation without just competitors.'

The announcement of the honour was made in 1806 and William resigned his seat in the House of Commons, though it was not until February, 1807, that he decided to relinquish his office at the Board of Agriculture. He sent in his resignation on 18 February, and had an instant reply from the Board's President, Sir John Sinclair:

> My dear Lord, Before your favour of the current reached me, I was under the necessity of circulating the names of the persons I wished to be appointed Ordinary Members, and considering our long acquaintance and habits of intimacy and friendship, I could not deny myself the pleasure of including you in the number. I really must remonstrate against the plan of your leading too retired a life. Your visiting London occasionally and amusing yourself with that sort of business which the Board of Agriculture furnishes, I am satisfied would be highly conducive to your health, to which nothing contributes more than a change of scene, and useful, without exhausting occupation ...

Lord Beauchamp, however, had more than sufficient to occupy his time. He had new properties, of course, some inherited, some newly purchased; of his ten surviving children, eight were to require complicated marriage settlements; but even more important was the necessity of warding off unwelcome suitors, for as Lord Redesdale wrote to a friend: 'I believe an union with the Beauchamp family is a sincere subject of congratulation'. There were mortgages to be renegotiated; an interesting list of debtors from Jennens' lawyers indicates who might be regarded as a good risk and who were unlikely to be reliable. There was a considerable amount of refurbishing of Madresfield Court, and several new London residences to be furnished; his eldest son had gone in 1801 and 1804 on tours to Scotland to meet the local aristocracy and their daughters, and then to the Continent in 1817 and 1820 to make the Grand Tour. His second son (who, although no one could have guessed it, was to become the third earl) was rather a disappointment, in that he insisted on marrying, in 1813, a lady from Co. Kilkenny of whom Catherine disapproved, whose family may have acquired some erstwhile Denne lands (see p.26)

The family also now developed an interest in collecting fine art, furniture and luxury objects, fostered by Catherine. Catherine bought fine art in Paris, and both the first and second earls bought fine art in both London and Paris. William, the eldest son and second earl, is credited in particular with the collection of historical portraits at Madresfield Court, and he also acquired both French and Italian furniture on the Continent, sending it home by sea to Bristol and then by the river Severn to Worcester. Though much has subsequently been sold, the cumulative effect of all their activities can be somewhat overpowering. There is an ornate pair of gold and turquoise earrings which are said to have belonged to Marie Antoinette; the last Countess Beauchamp tried to wear them once but pronounced them far too heavy for modern ears. And, supremely beautiful, there is a large collection of miniatures.

For most of the first earl's life the various wars elsewhere in Europe provided a dark backcloth. The atrocities of the French Revolution were said 'to have driven William Lygon from Whiggism into the Tory camp' and there are many stories of preparations against invasion. The incident of French troops landing at Fishguard in 1798 is well known—the last occasion when British soldiers fought foreigners on home soil. The somewhat fevered atmosphere of the time is brought to life by a hurriedly pencilled note on the inside front cover of one of William's ledgers—perhaps he was spending Sunday quietly making up his accounts:

> Sunday, Sep. 6, 1807. 2 o'Clock saw Two Men pass together of suspicous [sic] appearance the first about 5 five [sic] seven very sallow and dark complexion rather puny looking with thin features dark brown coat black stocking and a band over his shoulder, the other short and thick beard pale face stooped very much walked slowly with a check jacket much worn dirty and ill looking the first between 38/40 the other much younger probably little more than 20.

The note is reproduced exactly as written; the hasty scribble and the mistakes say much for William's agitation. Madresfield Court was very isolated; although quite effectively protected by its wide and deep moat, it stood alone amongst many acres of farmland, and even the nearest cottages, where some employees lived, were at a considerable distance. The fear of invasion or of local violence would have been coupled with appreciation that it was common knowledge that the newly created Baron Beauchamp of Powyke was spending money both on fine silver for the house and jewellery for his wife and six daughters. There would be fine pickings for any gang which could gain access to the house. In fact, the family were to find that the greatest danger came from dishonest staff; there was more than one incident of a thieving valet or a greedy lady's maid. That imposing moat was no defence against the enemy within.

The few letters written by Catherine give a contrasting picture of a lively personality combined with a very down to earth character. Here is a draft in her own hand, undated and unaddressed, which shows her as she wished her circle to see her:

> This is the first moment I could summon courage to express the misery I feel at the Melancholy tidings you sent me, of the dear Baron of [illegible], indeed, I thought from his state of insensibility, his case very desperate. My heart is almost broke, he had a thousand good qualities, though certainly nine hundred singularities. I feel great anxiety to hear how he departed this life; whether he made confession of his Numerous wicked projects against the fair - whether he mentioned me, and for what sum his executor sold his wardrobe. Every circumstance concerning a friend so very highly esteemed, must be interesting, and I must acknowledge I carry my curiosity and attention so far, that I wish to know what passage he had over the Styx, whether he crossed in a flat bottom'd or a [illegible] boat, if he was sick etc. - whether Charon is an able navigator. If the dear Baron was alive, I should blush to express all

these ancieties [*sic*], but to you, who were acquainted with his work, and loved him as yourself, whatever concern'd him. - It is my intention to be in London on Wednesday Evening - Mrs Andres gives a great gala on Thursday - of course you are invited, besides being <u>an excellent dancer</u>, your Star and ribbon will add great Splendour to the entertainment. Did you ever hear anything so shocking as the Murder of the Duke d'Anghuise? He was very brave and amiable, and died most nobly. - Good God, that such a Monster as Buonaparte should be permitted to live in this civilized country. Adieu Dear Gen'l and Mighty Baron! remember I am always visible until half past two o'clock. C.L. Sun. Morn.

But Catherine's letters—at least those which have been preserved—usually have a more serious intent. Soon after her two young sons had gained commissions in the army, she wrote to the Prince Regent on their behalf. Unfortunately, for it was no doubt a model of its kind, her letter has been lost, but she received a very satisfactory reply from his secretary:

> Sir Benjamin Bloomfield is commanded by the Prince Regent to assure Lady Beauchamp that His Royal Highness felt particular gratification in acknowledging the Merits of Her Ladyship's Sons, and His Royal Highness, in manifesting His Estimation of those two young Officers, has derived Satisfaction from the Communication of Lady Beauchamp. Lady Beauchamp quite overrates Sir Benjamin Bloomfield's attention, in which he hopes never to be deficient where the wishes of Her Ladyship demand his humble service.

Both sons eventually became generals.

But Catherine was above all an excellent housekeeper, as her letters to her husband show. She spent far more time in London than he did, and often entertained friends at the house in Belgrave Square which had been one of their first purchases with the Jennens inheritance. For instance, she writes to William with much underlining of her instructions, the week before she is to give a dinner party:

> If you can send up by the Coach <u>next Saturday</u>, not an hour before, 1 good Pine [apple] and plenty of Garden stuff and some pigeons, it will be acceptable here <u>next Sunday</u>, but the weather is so hot, <u>don't</u> send the basket before Saturday. <u>No Fowls</u>. Take great care of the swan's mate. Please write me word about <u>what</u> painting is doing. Are the coals and the bricks come? Is Jackson at Leigh? Have <u>new</u> Iron barrs put in the coppers in the Scullery, have that done <u>now</u>. I will write when I will have them done up by Jackson. Ever Yrs. C[atherine] B[eauchamp].

One hopes she is pleased to see swans still nesting on the moat—the prospect of being haunted by a displeased Catherine is somewhat daunting, but so far Madresfield has no tradition of a ghost.

She also protected her husband from his own good nature, as her way of dealing with a begging letter shows, when an acquaintance she considered unreliable asked for a loan:

> My dear L[ygon] ... The day before yesterday I received the enclosed letter, which I very civilly answered that I lamented it was not in my power to accommodate him. I might have said I could not lend money without <u>your</u> knowledge, but then I was affraid [*sic*] if I involved <u>your</u> name he might write and plague <u>you</u>. A fine, troublesome acquaintance.

On his ennoblement in 1806, William Lygon had of course to resign his Parliamentary seat, and it was not until 1810 that his eldest son could seek to regain the right to represent the county. But in that year, though only 23 years old—the earliest date at which he could stand—young William succeeded in his bid, despite fierce competition. The view of the opposition was clearly expressed by a long ballad which gained some popularity at the time, of which a few verses are given below. It had many topical allusions which have little significance now, but it showed how local people in Worcestershire viewed recent developments in Madresfield:

> There was a rich man tho' 'tis not very common
> If People say true, he was rul'd by a Woman
> Who lectur'd so often on hoarding up pelf
> That he soon became stingy and mean as herself.
>
> Now it happen'd one day he was made a great Lord
> But no light of as how does my listing afford;
> Most People suppose, tho' it must not be told
> That the principal actor, was one Mr Gold.
>
> He the County of W —— having thirty years led
> Was resolved to place his sweet son in his stead
> My Lady most wisely fix'd on a Day
> That Billy his sweet pretty face should display.
>
> But sad to relate, when they came to the Town
> They found that sweet Willy could not be cram'd down,
> Without strong opposition from all ranks of Men
> Who ne'er wished to see Billy L— again!

In due course 'sweet Willy' was returned as the county's new M.P. but never became deeply involved in national politics. However, it could justly be said that Catherine Denne had won her first, though not her last Parliamentary election.

As one would expect, her letters to her children show her as a loving but far from indulgent mother. When her third son, Henry, was wounded quite severely in the Peninsular War, her letters reveal concern but also a determination that he must follow strictly all the doctors' instructions to ensure his complete recovery, and although because of damage to his right arm he was away from his regiment for some time, she was not to be coerced into encouraging any absence longer than necessary. She took a similarly firm line with her daughters; when one was widowed as a young mother with eleven children and scant financial support from her late husband's family, Catherine despatched her one unmarried daughter, made very much in her mother's image, not so much to be a support as a spur to facing up to her changed circumstances and the need to plan for her new life.

Catherine kept several notebooks, of varying interest. Her Commonplace Book is filled with wise sayings or little snippets from popular writers which could be introduced into conversation to demonstrate how well-read she was. There are half-empty books which contain riddles and rhymes, or anecdotes about prominent figures, or ballads and occasionally witty and slightly naughty poems, and of course a book of recipes collected over the years from various friends' housekeepers, and homely remedies for minor ailments which may well have worsened rather than cured the pain. One particular recipe, for 'curing a Cancer [i.e. ulcer] or sore mouth' is especially hair-raising, but one cannot doubt that Catherine would have had the determination to insist on the patient accepting the treatment:

William Lygon, First Earl Beauchamp by Sir William Beechey

> Take one ounce of rocke alum, two drachms of cochineal, four ounces of double refined lump sugar, pound and boil them in a quart of water, and when cold put into a bottle - Pour some of the above mixture into a phial, and add a sufficient quantity of oil of vitriol to make it as sharp as the best wine vinegar, or sharper, shake it well, until the fermentation be over, then cork it up for use. If the Cancer bleed or discharge much, dip a skewer into some oil of vitriol, and touch the place so affected. Mix an equal quantity of sweet oil, and of the above mixture without oil of vitriol and make it as hot as can be borne, wrap a fine linen rag round a skewer, dip it therein, and dress the sore with it, also dress it with tincture of myrrh, and then with the sharp mixture, applied in the same manner. Dip some lint in the tincture of myrrh, squeeze it well touch it lightly with the sharp mixture, & lay over the first lint. Spread a little Fuller's earth on a piece of black silk, and stick it on the lint, to hinder it from dropping off. Dress round the sore with the oil, or tincture, or sharp mixture, before you open it. The sharp mixture alone will cure any sore mouth. It may be used for children with perfect safety - If the bone be bare, dress it with the juice or powder of angelica root, to make the flesh grow, and take away the pain caused by the sharp mixture.

Most of the recipes are for various economies, which might be thought surprising since by 1808, the date this book commenced, the Jennens inheritance was 10 years old, but Catherine with her large family had no doubt learned the need for thrift by bitter experience. For instance, there is:

> A Receipt for Cheap Paint - Take four pounds of Roman vitriol, and pour on it a teakettle full of boiling water: when dissolved, add two pounds of peal ash, and stir the mixture well with a stick, until the effervescence ceases, then add a quarter of a pound of pulverised yellow arsenic, and stir the whole together; let it be laid on, with a paint or whitewash brush, and if the wall has not been painted before, two or even three coats will be requisite. To paint a common sized room with this colour, will not cost more than five or six dollars. If a pea green is required put in less, and if an apple green more, of the yellow arsenic.

Evidently these instructions were imported but some of her culinary recipes indicate a more aristocratic origin. She has included 'Lord King's Sauce for cold Fowls or Game or salad' and 'The Waterford receipt for pickling Salmon' and there are some Continental sauces. But undoubtedly the most economical of all her suggestions is:

> A Receipt for Scarcity of Eggs: Bottle snow water, instead of Corks cover the top with paper and punch holes into it; it is excellent for Puddings instead of Eggs and will keep all the year. 2 or 3 spoonfuls is sufficient for a dish, it answers very well for Pancakes in place of Eggs.

So much for what her personal letters show. But was William sometimes irritated by his capable, managing wife? Did he ever grow tired of her driving ambition? On the other hand, perhaps that bright, intelligent face maintained the spell that had led to their marriage. Yet there was little to indicate the deeper feelings of either in the main body of their letters. However, the answer was found in a brief note sent by William when Catherine was obliged to stop overnight at Oxford when returning from one of her business trips. General Henry, the most untidy of her sons, and also the most sentimental, had preserved the small sheet of paper amongst his army records. It is dated 1 November, 1803, and the courtly language of an earlier century veils, without totally concealing, the evidence that this marriage between quiet, astute landowner and capable, ambitious woman, was a perfect partnership. He wrote:

> My dear Mrs Lygon, This being the 23rd anniversary of the day on which I had the honour of receiving your fair hand, I cannot let it pass without the sincerest congratulations both to you and myself and hearty wishes for the continuance of that domestic happiness we have so uniformly and undisputedly enjoy'd. I have only to add our best wishes for your safe and speedy return and I am, my dear Mrs L., very affectionately, W. Lygon.

This partnership continued happily for almost 14 more years, but its end was tragic. On Saturday, 19 October, 1816, less than a year after he had been advanced from Baron to Earl Beauchamp of Powyke, William Lygon left Madresfield for London, to be present at the wedding on the Monday of his fifth daughter, Georgiana Emma Charlotte, to Thomas, second Earl of Longford, the occasion which had prompted Lord Redesdale's comment on the desirability of 'an union with the Beauchamp family'—quite true, since the Longford finances were in a rather precarious state. On the Sunday night William retired to bed apparently in perfect health. About 3 a.m. Catherine was awakened by a groan as he lay beside her. He had expired in a fit of apoplexy. 'It is somewhat singular that the death of his Lordship's father was almost equally sudden', commented one newspaper. It was a pattern which was to be repeated more than once.

The wedding was, of course, postponed for three months. But the funeral itself took time to arrange, and it was not until the morning of Tuesday, 29 October, that 'at half-past six o'clock the remains of Lord Beauchamp were removed in a hearse with six horses, from his residence in St. James's Square. The hearse was followed by two mourning coaches and four horses, in which were some of his domestics; his Lordship's carriage and four closed the procession. On Saturday, 2 November, the body was interred in a mausoleum at Madresfield which his Lordship erected some years previously. The coffin was covered with red crimson velvet with silver gilt furniture.' But although William had indeed had the foresight to build a mausoleum, he had omitted to have it consecrated, and although this was not a legal requirement Catherine may have felt it desirable, and this could have contributed to the delay in his burial.

Catherine rarely visited Madresfield after her husband's death, although she was slow to relinquish her involvement in the management of the estates, especially during the comparatively brief incumbency of her eldest son. However, after his death she confined herself to her own property at Spring Hill, near Broadway, and to her residence in St. James' Square, London during the Season (May to September) and wintered in Paris. She died in London some 27 years later, on 2 March, 1844, when she was 80 years old, and was finally laid to rest beside her husband at Madresfield.

William and Catherine had 12 children, of whom one died in infancy. Three of their four sons succeeded in turn to the title and feature in the following chapters. Two of the other children merit a special mention here.

Edward Pyndar Lygon (1786-1860) was educated at Westminster School, joined the 2nd Regiment of Life Guards aged 17 and had a distinguished military career. As Lieutenant-Colonel he commanded the regiment at Waterloo when he was only 29 years old, and later became Colonel of the 13th Light Dragoons. He was subsequently made a Commander of the Bath.

He was a quiet and reserved man, unlike the traditional idea of a successful soldier. It was he who was always called upon to settle disagreements, and he who was the favourite uncle of the next generation. He never married, but when his sister Georgiana, Countess of Longford, was widowed in 1835 he is said to have unofficially adopted one of her sons as his heir (see the story of Charles Reginald Pakenham on pp.66). An apparently well-founded tradition has it that when after Waterloo Wellington offered Edward a decoration second class, it was promptly rejected with the words 'First class or nothing'. It seems that on that occasion Edward got nothing.

Like his elder brother General Henry, General Edward hid a very emotional nature under the mask of the professional soldier. He left one small pocket diary for the year 1847, in which his favourite niece died in childbirth. On the day of the funeral, returning to London by train, he wrote one simple entry: 'F's funeral. This is the saddest day of my life,' and the page is blotted with tears.

Lady (Jemima Catherine) Louisa Lygon (1791-1864) was known always as Lady Louisa, even within the family. The fifth daughter of William and Catherine Lygon, she had a strong personality and was held in great respect by all her relations. To her nephews and nieces any invitation to visit her at her London residence in Brook Street had the force of a royal command; sometimes in their letters they even refer to her as 'Aunt Lady Louisa'. After her father's death, when her brother the second earl resided at Madresfield, she acted as his hostess (neither was married), and chatelaine of the Court. It was in this capacity that she set up on her own initiative a savings scheme mainly for the domestic servants. They might contribute as little as threepence per week, which she banked for them so that in an emergency they might have a small sum available. She also became, though not in any great way, a tea trader. She arranged for chests of tea to be sent from London to the tenant of Hayswood Farm, close to the Court, and the tenant sold small quantities locally on her behalf.

After the second earl's death, Lady Louisa returned to live in London for the rest of her life. She was a wealthy woman and, anxious to make good use of her fortune, she proposed to build almshouses near Madresfield for local people in their old age. However, this wish was negated by the desire of her sister-in-law, wife of the third earl, who left a considerable sum for the same purpose (see p.77). Lady Louisa therefore donated a piece of land which she had inherited in Chelsea, and on this were built eventually the Lygon Almshouses, which came unscathed through two wars. One feels that even Hitler was deterred by the stern ghost of Lady Louisa. The 'Lygon Almshouses' as they were named, still survive and they and the charity which administers them have been adapted successfully to modern needs.

The Lygon Almshouses. Various stones preserved within the complex record that the original almshouses were founded in 1833 and rebuilt in 1886. A further development took place in 1906, since when they have all been rebuilt

CHAPTER SIX
William, Second Earl Beauchamp (1782-1823)

William was the second child of William and Catherine Denne; their first, a daughter, died as a young woman (her memorial tablet is in Exeter Cathedral). He was educated at Westminster School and Christ Church, Oxford. Apart from two journals he kept, covering two tours in Scotland, he left very few records.

He was only 18 when he went on his first tour of Scotland in the summer vacation of 1801, travelling with a tutor, Mr Walsh, and Thomas, a groom from Madresfield. His father had instructed him to take good note of any developments in methods of agriculture and in farm buildings, but this seems not to have held much appeal for the young man, for he wrote only one letter which briefly refers to the subject. He was perhaps more interested in the residences of his hosts, probably because alterations to Madresfield Court were coming under consideration. His mother, however, realising the advantages of their recent Jennens inheritance, was anxious that her eldest son should become acquainted with as many of the Scottish aristocracy, especially their daughters, as soon as possible. Young William undoubtedly enjoyed this behest, so much so that when the 'noble lords', as he calls them, came north from London at the end of August he seems to have abandoned his sight-seeing in favour of the social round.

He travelled throughout on horseback, and leaving London on 29 June rode from London via Oxford, Birmingham, Liverpool and Lancaster to Carlisle. The critical comments of his journal are indicative of what was to come: In Carlisle:

> I was much disappointed, the Principal Buildings being built of a reddish kind of Sand Stone which gives them a very sombre appearance ... The Castle is still extremely perfect ... The Garrison consists at present of 7 old men, I conjecture to guard the Stores that are kept in a Tower which is quite Perfect ... Mr Law (one of the Prebends) obligingly went with me to see the Cathedral which I should suppose is very near the worst in England ... Perhaps its deficiency in Ornament may be from its being situated in a frontier Town, continually exposed to the attacks of the Turbulent Scotchmen.

William went on through Hamilton and Kilwilling to Saltcoats and Stavenson

> mostly inhabited by the Workmen belonging to the Neighbouring Collieries. These supply the export trade between Irvine and Dublin, to the amount of 17 or 18,000 tons annually, but the Long distracted situation of that unhappy Country has totally interrupted the distilleries and Manufactories which demanded the Coal from this Coast, so that many of the Collieries are now entirely stopped. Vessels pass from hence to Arran three times a week.

His strictures upon the Scots were somewhat moderated a couple of days later,

> ... when a heavy rain came on and obliged me to pass hastily through the Village of Dalrymple, from the transient view of the scenery of the River, it seemed to deserve the deliberate notice of the Curious Traveller, but tho' disappointed here my pleasure was soon derived from a different source. From the sullen answers returned to my civil questions I had till this imagined that what I had seen in Various Tourists of the civility of the Lower Order of Scotsmen was totally void of Foundation or at least that a great alteration had lately taken place, but all these unfavourable ideas now gave way to more just ones by the kindness with which I was received in a cottage to which I galloped for Shelter. The Poor man hearing we had not yet dined immediately dispatched his wife for the family Stores, of which we partook heartily, and at our departure it was with the greatest difficulty we gained our point of returning some small present for their civility and hospitality.

And so to Glasgow

> a large well built town ... The Tontine Buildings ... consist of an Hotel and a large Coffee Room which has 600 Subscribers who meet here regularly to read the papers and settle their political Affairs. Strangers are admitted Gratis ... The High Church is situated on a rising ground. Its immediate vicinity was formerly the abode of the dignified Clergy etc. but is now inhabited by the Lower Classes ... The Green is extremely spacious. In it is a public Washing House to which whoever pleases brings Cloaths to wash. Hot Water they have Gratis, the Boilers being supplied from the River. This Novelty has a pleasing Effect, particularly on a fine day, when the Cloaths are spread out.

On the following Sunday, having seen 'vast quantities of People passing towards the Ferry from an early hour', he discovered it was Sacrament Sunday, which happened once a year at Luss, and joined the throng.

> From Inveruglass to Luss is three miles and the whole way was crouded with Whiskies, Carts, Horse and Foot, every one in his Sunday dress. The day was uncommonly fine and it reminded me strongly of Piccadilly when crouded with Hyde Park visitors. At our arrival we found not only the Kirk as full as it could hold, but also two Priests (one of whom was the celebrated Mr Stewart the translator of the Bible into Gaelic)

haranguing in the Yard to an immense and attentive Audience. The Village is prettily situated on the banks of the Lake. It has a small Inn, by no means so commodious as one ought to be to which such crouds resort every Summer.

His next stop was with the Duke of Argyll at Inveraray Castle, where

Most of the Female Servants were barefooted which would have surprized me greatly, had I not been prepared for it by seeing the same thing at Hamilton Palace.

He went on to a miserable expedition to the island of Mull, then to Iona and Staffa, and back to Mull for the trip to Oban. But misfortune still dogged him. The boat left port at nightfall,

and with nothing to amuse the eye, my cold and weary fellow Travellers forgot all their Cares in a peaceful Sleep. In this situation of inconvenience that niceness of disposition which home encourages was quickly laid aside. The Filthy bottom of the Boat was gladly substituted for down, and a dirty Seaman's coat was seized for a covering. The Night though cold was calm and pleasant, no sound was heard except reiterated snores from the bottom of the Boat which supplied food for Laughter not only to me, but to the Sailors. Not disposed to follow the example set me, I chatted away with some of the boatmen who understood English, who among other information gave me to understand that Mr Pitt was shortly expected at Staffa. At their requite I gave a description of his person lest among other Casual Visitors he might slip by unobserved, and in return I was treated with several love songs, the melody of which is wild and sweet. We did not land till three o'clock in the morning. Nor was misfortune yet tired of persecuting us. Two of our party not sufficiently alert in following the Captain of the Boat lost their way and did not arrive at the Inn till long after us, and at their arrival found their Apartment occupied by a fury whom neither Supplication nor Threat could dislodge. It may not be amiss to observe that under the pretence of Madness, this woman extorts money which is in general gladly given in order to get rid of her Persecution. But my harassed Fellow Travellers were too much fretted by their fatigue to use this mode of purchasing Rest, and the Master of the House having at last silenced her, we retired to rest at four o'clock.

William set out for Oban the following evening, but apparently having missed the tide had to return to Mull about 2 a.m. and

with some difficulty we got ashore and were conducted by one of the Crew to a miserable Publick House. Two Beds were in the room we were ushered into, three men occupying one and the Landlord, his Wife and a flock of children the other. No Bed was therefore to be obtained, but through the care of my Servant I was provided with a door, on which supported by two Chairs I had a tolerably comfortable Nap. At six o'clock we embarked ... about ten o'clock we were landed at Oban tired and exhausted for want of Rest and food.

He must indeed have been exhausted, for here the journal breaks off and the rest of the tour is described in letters to his mother.

In these letters he expresses much more frankly his opinions of his hosts, and sometimes records with satisfaction how little the tour is costing. For instance, he writes from Inverness:

> My horses do very well which is extremely lucky. Mine is so good a one that if it does knock up I shall leave Thomas to ride it up to Madresfield. I have already saved by purchasing them, I mean the Hire would have been more than the purchase Money.

He learned one day of the death of the Marquess of Aberdeen:

> Ld Aberdeen's riches make as much noise in Scotland as Mr Jennens' did in England ... Ld Haddo [the heir] is left by no means well. He has the Entailed Estate ... almost all the rest goes to Natural Children.

A few days later he goes shooting:

> ... here a good Shot never goes out without killing 50 brace. [At Duneira] We had another Earthquake last night just as we were gone to Bed, I thought it bad enough but was assured it was hardly anything, however, it rocked my bed about as if I had been in a Cradle.

But he had something more important than his experience of an earthquake to tell his mother. He had met with two French Royals, and at first he was favourably impressed: 'The French Princes seem extremely good natured ... They are making the Tour of Scotland alone in a Curricle - with only two or three Servants ...' But only two days later William had changed his mind:

> I don't like [the Duke of Orléans] at all, as he seems a dark ill-looking Frenchman. Monsieur de Beaupolez is a very lively good natured young man, too young to have joined in any of his father's Wickednesses ... All Ayrshire is amazingly outrageous at Lord Capilis, who slipped away from Cullean, that he might not receive the French Princes. It was very wrong as in consequence of their hearing he was at home but a few hours before, their plans were so discomposed as to oblige them to sleep in a small public House at Maybole. I suppose it was his Stingyness ... The French Princes are going back to Edinburgh. They are extremely goodnatured, but very great boares [sic]. The Youngest is deeply smitten with Lady Georgiana to her very great annoyance.

William's last comment on Scotland on this occasion is in another letter to his mother on 26 September:

> I am very sorry to leave the Highlands. I am sure I shall not be able to sleep the first night for sorrow. I think I have now got well acquainted with the Northern Powers.

So much for the 18-year-old William Lygon. Three years later he returned to tour Scotland, travelling this time up the east coast. He kept a journal of this, but only for about the first three weeks, and no letters to his parents have been preserved. The years since his first visit evidently made a striking difference in the young man's perception of all things Scottish, and he now maintains a very critical attitude indeed. In Hawick:

> the Houses are miserable and dirty ... its inhabitants, judging from their squalid appearance only, nearly bordering on a state of Starvation ... Selkirk is also abominably filthy and disgusting and its Houses apparently in a most dilapidated state. Some Travellers may take fright at the badness of the accommodations and therefore may suffer their judgements to be warped by that Casual Circumstance - I am not difficult to be pleased, therefore that cannot be my motive, but I will not hesitate to pronounce it as bad as bad can be and the sooner a Traveller gets out of it the better for him ... The Inn is not so bad as many Travellers have represented it ... I ought not to praise my accommodations too much as from the Rottenness of the Floor of my Apartment, which is the best in the House, I have been within an ace of paying a visit to a noisy party in the Kitchen, unexpected and uninvited.

He viewed Edinburgh itself on this second visit with some disillusion, principally because of new houses built in a situation which ruined his previously 'highly prized Prospect'. It was apparently the wrong time of year for a young man to be visiting Scotland's capital city, for

> The Edinburgh Season begins in January and ends in April. Unless at that time, the Town is deserted and the Streets are covered with Grass and Weeds.

From Edinburgh he retraced the steps of his former tour to Oban, Mull and other islands. But his interest now centred more on the economics of Scottish life, and he shows concern for the plight of the small farmers and their consequent

> wish to attempt the dangerous experiment of trying their fortunes in America ... The last step of government was a prudent one, and has tended very materially to check emigration for the present, as under the appearance of providing for their comfort on the passage, the price is encreased [*sic*] to twenty Guineas, a sum which few with families can afford to pay.

Since Dr. Samuel Johnson's visits to Scotland had been the inspiration for many of William's contemporaries (not to mention himself) to follow suit, there is a certain hint of smugness in his remark after seeing Staffa that

> neither Dr Johnson or Mr Pennat were at Staffa, the latter had a great desire to visit it but the prudence of Mr Thompson the Master of his vessel prevented him from gratifying it.

At Strontian he found an early example of a prefab:

> The Inn was originally wholly of wood, and was brought from London ready cut out, and had only to be put together when it arrived. It has now been surrounded with Stone, and is (considering the wild Countryside in which it is placed and the uncertainty of its business) a decent House, in spite of all I had heard to the contrary.

From Strontian he had difficulty in reaching Coran Ferry,

> at the Mouth of Loch Eil. The Rocks for about two miles are almost perpendicular to the Sea, and this can only be passed by a horse at low Water. There is a foot Path among the rocks. We now came to a River, Broad Deep and Rapid. I think its name is Goer ... The Strontian Beast had to make many journeys backwards and forwards as without the assistance of his mane and tail we never could have crossed at all. The Man who presided over the baggage horse took us over one by one. I don't know how my friends fared but he pinched me so immoderately in order to hold on fast, that I have very considerable doubts whether I ever shall lose the impressions of his kindness. Had we been a very short time later, I doubt whether we could have crossed it at all.

The last entry in this journal, dated 11 August, 1804, deals with his experience of Glencoe:

> The Road for some distance was tolerably level on the banks of the Coe, which abounds with trout. The morning had till this been tolerably fine, but it now rained furiously and to add to the general Misfortunes the torrents of water which had descended from the Mountains on the preceding day, had made very considerable chasms in the road, which had not been put in a state of complete repair above a few days. We were obliged once to take the Horses from the Carriages and to drag them over ourselves with some difficulty ... There is but one House within the distance of 9 miles, and the heath affords pasture only to a few Goats. I found it by far the most miserable Inn I ever met with ... After fires had been lighted by which we might dry ourselves, the enquiries naturally turned upon the road we were to pursue to fort William; when to our very great surprize it was discovered that the roads we had expected to find fit for Carriages were impassable even for Horses; and that our best plan was to return to Balhuilis as expeditiously as possible. We had some time necessarily to stay while the horses were feeding, the next interrogations were as to the state of the larder. No Meat, No Milk, No Eggs, No Bread. This negative was repeated so frequently that I now had a serious idea that it was the only English word in the possession of our hostess, but at length to my great joy to the enquiry whether there were any Hens, an affirmative was given ... When they appeared before us, they were as might easily have been expected tough and indigestible. There was no temptation to remain here longer than was unavoidable. A Servant had been dispatched with directions to prepare dinner at Balhuilis. It was dark when we arrived there, and we found a very civil message from Capt Stewart (whose House is not a hundred yards from the

Inn) to say he had two Beds at our Service. There were but four Beds in the Inn, his kind offer was therefore eagerly accepted in order that the Servants might profit by it -

The journal breaks off here, but there are a few sheets of a rough draft of William's journey to Inverness and Sutherland. From a list of places visited, it seems likely that from then on William's purpose was mainly a round of social visits. His thirst for adventure had been satisfied, so far as Britain was concerned. In 1817 and 1820 he travelled on the Continent, where he collected historical portraits and small *objets d'art*, an activity he also pursued in London, buying china, plate, books, sculpture and miniature boxes.

He became Member of Parliament for Worcestershire in 1810 and so remained until he succeeded to the title in October 1816, when he was 34 years of age. The only Parliamentary occasion on which he attracted considerable notice, mostly favourable, was when the House of Commons debated whether to discuss the alleged misdemeanours of Princess Caroline, whose husband, the Prince Regent, wanted a divorce. One of her most vocal defenders was young William Lygon who, in order to prevent disclosure of details of the adultery with which she was charged, on the grounds of respect for the Crown, threatened that whenever the matter was raised he would use the traditional cry of 'I spy strangers!' to disrupt the House. Despite heated objections by his opponents, his threat produced at least temporarily his desired result.

After his succession to the title, William seems to have devoted his time more to his own interests than to politics. He took with enthusiasm to the life of a wealthy landowner. With his eldest sister, Lady Louisa, as his hostess, he became famous as a generous host to the whole county. He showed a keen interest in the management of the estates, but was obliged to depend to a very great extent on the experience of Jarvis Arnold, (see below) who had been appointed bailiff by the first earl in about 1799 and probably had a more intimate knowledge of how Madresfield operated than any of his employers.

William seems to have alienated his siblings by his autocratic attitude, writing especially to his sisters in terms that his father never used. 'I desire that this shall be done without failing ... I am peremptory in this' is an instruction that appears more than once. His brother Edward typically tried to keep in touch with him, but even he was rebuffed on occasion.

Yet there is a letter from Jarvis Arnold to Edward which suggests that William may have needed his family's support more than he would admit. All his life William seems to have distanced himself from his immediate family, over-conscious of his position as its head, and eventually facing an early death in great loneliness. But he would be a generous host when his position called for it. So Arnold could write to another of William's brothers, Henry, in July 1818 after a number of civic dignitaries had been entertained at the Court:

> Yesterday was the most convivial day that ever have [*sic*] been seen at Madresfield for a number of years, and his Lordship seemed highly Gratified and passed the Compliment that it went off extremely well - which of course was a Gt. Satisfaction to us. Drank a wonderful deal of Wine. The Mayor of Evesham properly cut up - the high

Two portraits of the Hon. Edward Lygon, youngest brother of the second earl

Bailiff and the rest of the Corporation of Kidderminster very jovial - the Corporate [*sic*] of Worcester the same - the sentiments and songs given were fine - the Hero's [*sic*] of Salamanca and Waterloo with 3 times three. The Greatest part of the Corporation of Kidderminster was particularly Jovial and proper John Bulls. When they went off in their open Carriages [they] went singing along - Good Queen Bes's [*sic*] Golden Days - and seemed so highly Gratified with their Host and Entertainment - and I hope in God they all arrived safe home. Never men seemed so highly Pleased and Gratified.

But as the years passed William became more and more withdrawn, and began eventually to live the life of a recluse at Madresfield, surrounded by some of the treasures he had collected, and relying very largely on Lady Louisa to carry out his orders regarding the estate.

He had already shown during his Scottish tour in 1801 a close regard to due economy in expenditure, and he had proudly reported to his mother on how little his travels had cost him. That trait now became somewhat exaggerated. He maintained the tradition of New Year gifts for all the employees, but his written instructions to Lady Louisa on the subject have an ungenerous flavour. In writing which by this time was so minute as to be almost indecipherable even with the aid of a magnifying glass, he wrote just after his last Christmas, which he had apparently spent in London, ordering his sister to give 'old

Purser not a thing, an old rascal; the wife what you like ... Bond nothing whatever excepting a rope if this is of any use to hang himself.' But the venom of such remarks is countered by the detailed attention in a long list of gifts to be made to a number of employees and noting their individual needs: 'Mrs ...: Bed Gown, Petticoat, Flannel do. Shift' is an entry repeated many times, until one comes to 'Old Stokes: A Shirt; Young Mrs Stokes Bed gown, Petticoat, Flannel do. Shift; That Beast Stokes: Shirt.' The list resumes without comment until 'Young Slaughter's wife Complete [i.e. Bed Gown, etc.] unless she cants [complains] and then to be sent about her business.' But as there are more than 40 names in all, probably he may be forgiven a few displays of something less than goodwill, especially since he was already terminally ill. He concludes in his inimitable style 'I desire nothing is given away but I order; <u>upon this I am peremptory</u>. If any others suggest themselves to you let me know and I will tell you what to give if they are not disagreeable.'

There is just one more sad little note, undated but now in minuscule writing: 'My dear Louisa, One day passes so like another, that I have nothing to say. I am not gaining ground in my health, and am uncommonly weak in my knees.'

He died on 13 May 1823, only 40 years of age. Whatever his failings, there were some who held him in high regard, and the newspapers printed their tributes. Lady Louisa apparently masterminded his funeral, an occasion the like of which Worcestershire had never seen. At Madresfield Court his remains

> lay in state in the Grand Saloon which was entirely hung with superfine black cloth ... The inside coffin was lined with rich white satin, frilled and ruffled and the dress elegantly trimmed with the same; the leaden coffin was inclosed in one of English oak, covered with rich crimson Genoa velvet and furnished in the handsomest manner with silver furniture and every appropriate decoration ... At each end of the coffin, upon stands covered with black cloth, stood an elegant silver branch with 3 large wax lights, which with other lights disposed around the room gave it a most solemn and imposing effect ...

according to *Berrow's Journal*, and the funeral itself was a scene of similar grandeur. The use of several coffins was partly to deter grave robbers; although the practice of stealing corpses for dissection by medical students was prevalent mainly in the big cities, the fear of such desecration was widespread also amongst those who divided their time between London and the country.

The Bailiff

Letters of the rich and famous are a valuable source of information about the lives and times of their writers. Equally valuable, but far less numerous, are the papers of their servants since so few of the humbler orders had sufficient education to express themselves on paper. Madresfield is fortunate to possess a small collection from a long-serving employee.

Jarvis Arnold's employment began in 1799. He was a young man who originated from Leeds and perhaps came to the Beauchamps by recommendation from the Adair family of Norfolk, close friends of Catherine Denne and bankers by occupation who had come to England from the north of Ireland; one or two references suggest that Arnold was familiar with the Adair household.

Jarvis Arnold was probably more influential than any other employee has been at Madresfield. Even the much better-known Victorian head gardener William Crump, honoured with the Gold Medal of the Royal Horticultural Society for his reconstruction of the gardens and grounds, never had quite as much freedom as Arnold to decide the fate of tenants and employees. He started as a very young bookkeeper and was soon appointed as bailiff, a position he held for the rest of his life.

His first love was calligraphy, and it is to this interest we chiefly owe his records. He begins with examples of what he calls 'fine penmanship', evidently under the supervision of a teacher: eulogies of Nelson, moral and uplifting extracts from books, and copies of sporting and other pictures from periodicals. In 1814 he notes that he paid two guineas for the 'binding of My Book of Penmanship in Russia Extra', and as fortunately he included with his scripts a considerable number of blank pages, this book developed into a detailed but confused journal of his personal as well as Lord Beauchamp's estate matters. The 'Russia Extra' is very worn now, and the key to its brass lock lost, but otherwise the record is undamaged.

Arnold's penmanship is also evident in the letters he wrote to Lady Beauchamp, who took a considerable share in the administration of the estates; and from the beginning Arnold had more correspondence with her than with her husband. He wrote in a large and very clear hand decorated with innumerable serifs and curlicues; his spelling was erratic, and his punctuation idiosyncratic—oblique strokes, for example, served sometimes as brackets, sometimes as quotation marks.

The first Earl Beauchamp expected the same high standards of accounting from his employees that he imposed on himself, and Catherine his wife was even stricter. After the earl's death, Arnold's correspondence was chiefly with her or with her daughter, Lady Louisa, who became executrix first for her father in 1816 and then for her eldest brother in 1832. She too expected the highest standards; letters following her brother's death, from their local solicitor, Mr. Turberville of Hanley Swan, show his anxiety to account for every last penny.

After a few years Arnold had as an assistant a Mr. Dawes who was something of a rival and did not hesitate to write direct to either the countess or Lady Louisa whenever he could find an excuse. Arnold therefore carefully noted every occasion on which he accepted Dawes' word as ground for action. For instance, they disagreed as to the date a new tenant entered on possession: Arnold thought it should have been Michaelmas (September) 1824, but Dawes insisted on Candlemass (February) 1825, so, reducing his ornate handwriting to a minuscule size, Arnold wrote in his Cash Book against the altered date: 'By what Mr Dawes says. NB This Cottage being in so bad a State, the [previous] Tenant run [sic] away from it, and [it] was uninhabit [sic] some time before it was repaired.' The amount forfeited by the alteration was £2. But Arnold knew his employer's passion for accuracy; a little later an entry records the division, according to acreages, of a rent received: £11 13s. in total—£3 11s. 9½d. to Lady Louisa and £8 1s. 2½d. to her mother.

Arnold learned his accounting skills from his employers, and since they delighted in preserving all their bank books, etc. Arnold too kept all his records. As he dealt with the properties not only of the earl and the countess, but also three of their children—the second earl, Lady Louisa and General Edward—as well as his own two private pocket-books in which he recorded his personal expenditure, there is quite a considerable amount of information. But nowhere does he give any hint as to his own wages, though these cannot have been very much, judging by amounts paid to other staff. Yet eventually he saved enough to buy himself a cottage in Malvern Link, about three miles away from the Court, on which he had to spend varying amounts in repairs over the next few years. It was about this time that he married, for he also spent a considerable sum on new clothes as well as furniture for the cottage, though it is several years before his first reference to 'my dear wife'.

But although he was now married, there was another innovation: each year he went on holiday, by himself, to London by invitation of the countess to stay at one of the London houses. The first record of such a holiday is in May, 1829, when his travelling expenses, including meals, both ways totalled just under £6. His amusements in London are in keeping with the character revealed in his other records: he visited picture galleries and bought several paintings and engravings; he arranged to have a quantity of wine 'sent by water from London'; he dined well on several occasions; heard a 'Charity Sermon' at St. James' Church which cost him 1s. 6d.; bought 3lb. Tea for £1 4s. But usually by far the most frequent entries relate to new clothes for himself: neckcloths 4s., handkerchief and neckcloth 4s. 3d., gloves and cap etc. 8s., new waistcoat 14s. The following year tobacco and snuff are included, but only 2lb. of tea for his wife, probably because there had been a sharp increase in cost. In 1831 he notes only the total he had spent on new clothes and an umbrella, plus the 2lb. of tea and rather inexplicably honey—perhaps he realised that his wife might need sweetening, since there is never any hint that she went away on holiday. At home, whilst Mrs. Arnold's housekeeping was regularly noted, bacon and cheese are regularly recorded under a separate heading. There is a strict division of expenses between those which he himself incurred, and amounts paid by him on behalf of his wife. What housekeeping allowance he gave her is not recorded, but any expenses he incurred which fell within her domain had to be duly reimbursed by her. For example, he had a regular supply of wines etc. from Stallard's in Worcester; he drank brandy, sherry and cider, but his wife preferred port. However, the charge for carriage from Worcester was equally divided. Presumably she also had a clothing allowance, for only his expenditure on his own attire is noted.

In 1832 there is a new and possibly ominous note about his London activities: 'Lost at cards 2/-' and later '4/6d.' In the following year he apparently entered details in a 'London small Book' which has vanished. Later he becomes increasingly concerned about his health, and there are recurring entries for the purchase of Physick, usually sarsaparilla and senna. But it is clear that Jarvis Arnold was beginning to climb the social ladder; expenditure on clothes was always an important item, and now covers 'oilskinning a Hat' (waterproofing?) and silver buckles for his best shoes. And locally he and his wife were now attended by the socially fashionable Dr. Garlike, no doubt through Lady Beauchamp's influence since the medical services were given free. However, Arnold made more than one present of game to the worthy doctor.

At the end of 1829 he had noted with equanimity that his total expenses for the year had been £117 11s. 1d. Twelve months later when the figure had risen to £172 4s. 11$^{1}/_{2}$d. he wrote in horror 'I trust and hope the Disbursements will never amt. again to the above sum.' Despite his successful economising in 1831, which reduced the total to £139 19s. 6$^{1}/_{2}$d. he repeated 'I hope and trust my next year's disbursements will prove much curtailed from the above amount.' He succeeded in reducing the figure to £130 12s. 10d. at the end of 1832, which evidently pleased him for here is no lament. But his satisfaction was not to be repeated. At the end of 1833 the total had shot up to £174 15s. 2$^{1}/_{2}$d. and the familiar hope reappears. The remainder of this book is taken up with a detailed account of 'Physic' purchased.

After the sudden death of the first earl in 1816, Countess Catherine relied on Arnold for information about her four sons' behaviour, particularly that of the second earl at Madresfield Court. There is a strange quality about these letters. Hers are very formal, sometimes written in the third person. They invariably begin with just 'Arnold ...' but are signed 'C.B.' as to other friends, though their tone is always one of command. His replies, in contrast, are occasionally quite informal. There is no suggestion that he ever played John Brown to her Queen Victoria, but there is no doubt that their relationship was quite close, and in his own quiet way he had as great a say in the management of the estate as his employers.

But with the death of Countess Catherine in 1844, Jarvis Arnold's influence began to wane, and he himself died very suddenly in 1846. Three weeks later his wife also died. For almost 48 years he had served the family faithfully, and it is difficult to consider Madresfield apart from him.

CHAPTER SEVEN
John Reginald (Lygon) Pindar, Third Earl Beauchamp (1783-1853)

John Reginald, second son of William and Catherine Lygon, was born on 21 November, 1783, educated at Westminster School, and matriculated at Christ Church, Oxford in 1802. The Madresfield muniments contain very little regarding his early life, and even less about his subsequent career. This hiatus is most probably due to the breach with the family in 1814 on his marriage to Lady Charlotte Scott, which apparently gravely damaged his relationship with his mother and to a lesser extent that with his siblings.

The reasons for this breach are not entirely clear. In 1813, the last member of that branch of the Pyndar family which owned considerable estates in Lincolnshire died, stipulating—as William Lygon of Madresfield had done in 1720—that any claimant must adopt a new surname, in this case, Pindar. Such a course was unthinkable for the first Earl Beauchamp and for his eldest son and heir. But John, now 30 years of age, was already planning marriage to a lady unpopular with his mother, and perhaps the prospect of providing him with an estate in Lincolnshire appeared a satisfactory solution to a delicate problem, since his bride seems to have in fact found no favour with any of the Lygon family. Whatever the reason, a claim to the Pindar estate was made in his name and in due course admitted. The grant of his new coat of arms was issued in the name of 'Pindar'—the Lincolnshire, not the Herefordshire, spelling of the name which had brought so much unhappiness to Margaret Lygon a hundred years previously, but the document carefully emphasised that he relinquished the Lygon surname only for himself and not for any descendants he might have.

On 14 March 1814, John duly married Lady Charlotte Scott, daughter of the first Earl of Clonmell, by special licence at St. Mary-le-bone Church in London, with which her family had connections. Lord Clonmell had had a distinguished career in law and, although his reputation was one of considerable eccentricity, he was Chief Justice of Ireland; her mother was the daughter and heiress of an Irish banker whose fortune was reputed to be immense. So far as lineage and finance were concerned, she would appear to have been very acceptable as a bride for a younger son. Yet in their correspondence

Catherine and at least two of her daughters exhibit considerable antipathy and contempt for her. Perhaps it was due to the fact that both Lord Clonmell and her mother came from families who had benefitted from the privileges accorded to English settlers in Ireland.

John made at least one attempt to heal the breach between himself and his mother. In June, 1833, he wrote to her on behalf of his wife as well as himself regretting the estrangement and asking for permission to visit. This letter may have been followed up by a formal visit, but there is no indication of any further improvement in the unhappy situation.

After his succession to the title following the death of his brother, John resided for much of his time at Madresfield Court and interested himself in agricultural matters, particularly in the living conditions of farm labourers. His succession coincided with the struggles of the Tolpuddle Martyrs and with forced emigration, and in the late 1830s, when floods and rains caused unprecedented unemployment in nearby Powick, he

St. Mary-le-bone Church in London

promoted an Emigration Fund to enable labourers to join the Worcestershire emigrants who were part of the new Colony of South Australia. He kept a strict control over rent increases, and arranged for Christmas gifts of coal to be hauled a distance of several miles over the Old Hills, between Malvern and Powick, to needy tenants in remote cottages on his estate, and later he developed a keen concern for education amongst his tenants and their children. John and his wife made a number of extended visits to the Continent, for like his brothers he was interested in collecting, though few of his purchases remain at Madresfield.

One example of his collecting passion caused immense irritation in Malvern. In 1831 the Duchess of Kent with her daughter, the 12 year-old Princess Victoria, who were staying at Holly Mount, honoured with their presence a charity bazaar held at the Royal Library, then housed in the building that is now Barclays Bank, at the junction of Edith Walk with the Worcester road. John attended and bought up for £5 all the pincushions made and contributed by the young princess, much to the annoyance of local ladies. What became of these needlework trophies is not known. Certainly one feels that the Lygons, of all collectors, would never willingly have let these slip through their fingers.

*Madresfield Court in the early 1860s.
Above, looking west to the Malverns, below looking northwards*

Charlotte brought with her a dowry of £60,000. This of course passed into her husband's control, but when she died on 26 April 1846, her husband honoured the promise he had made to her that it would be used for the building of almshouses at Newland, near Malvern, to be occupied by 'decayed agricultural labourers', although this work did not commence until after his own death. It is to be regretted that she whose money enabled this work has been so consistently forgotten. That John had agreed, at the time of their marriage, to Charlotte's request as to the use of her dowry, is known to have been a contributory factor in Catherine's dislike of her first daughter-in-law.

In 1850 John married again, to Catherine Braye, a widow whose father had been Henry Otway, a landowner in Co. Tipperary; perhaps it was just as well that his mother was no longer alive. John had no children by either wife. He had willed to be buried beside his first wife in St. Mary-le-bone, where there is an ornate memorial to him, yet the obituary notice in the *Worcester Herald* suggests a very different character from that depicted in the monument's extravagance:

> The dead nobleman, although a staunch Conservative, mixed himself up very little in political affairs and was better known as an unostentatious country gentleman than as a public character. With a certain degree of shyness of manner he was kind and courteous to all who approached him, and his tenantry unanimously accord to him the enviable but we hope not uncommon character of having been a considerate and liberal landlord.

Elsewhere he is described as 'the peasants' Earl' because of his unfailing concern for the poor.

In his will he left the majority of his personal estate to Lady Charlotte's nephew, Colonel Charles Grantham Scott, whom they regarded almost as their son. This bequest included part of the Lincolnshire estate, for the colonel's father had been disinherited by his father, the second Earl of Clonmell, and although he was heir presumptive to the title it was clear that his income would not sustain a lifestyle appropriate to the position. The Irish estate eventually went to another, and Colonel Scott's son, who many years later became sixth Earl of Clonmell, must have been grateful for John's thoughtfulness.

The *Worcester Herald* noted that 'The late Earl has left property to a value of upwards of £700,000 ... By his will the Earl has made Colonel Scott heir to all the landed estates not entailed with the [Beauchamp] title.' So the last link between Pindars and Madresfield was broken.

CHAPTER EIGHT
Henry, Fourth Earl Beauchamp (1785-1863)

The third son of William Lygon and Catherine Denne was born at Madresfield on 7 January 1785, and christened Henry Beauchamp Lygon. Like his brother he was educated at Westminster School, and matriculated at Christ Church, Oxford in 1803. Shortly afterwards he obtained a commission in the army, and subsequently served in the 13th and 16th Light Dragoons in the Peninsula War under Wellington. During the attempt to relieve Almeida in 1810, he was severely wounded, being shot in the throat. The bullet passed through his windpipe and was removed by a surgeon on the battlefield, without benefit of anaesthetic, and is still preserved at Madresfield. His colonel, Sir Willoughby Cotton, in reporting Henry's wound, described him as 'the most intimate friend I have and as gallant an officer as ever served'. At the same time Henry also received a wound in the arm which occasioned much concern and proved a continuing source of pain; he was convalescent for many months.

In 1815 he transferred to the 1st Life Guards, becoming closely involved in their formation and development, and whose Lieutenant-Colonel he was from 1821 to 1837, when he became Major-General.

In the library at Madresfield Court there is a book, *Tales of my Father*, published in 1902, written by a lady who used only her initials A.M.F., which has several references to a 'Lord B.', identified by the seventh Earl Beauchamp as his grandfather General Henry. She gives an interesting account of the impact on the Life Guards of the news that they had a new young sovereign in 1837:

> A report had spread that the King [William IV] was already dead, so Lord B., my father's colonel, ordered him to have all the horses saddled, and the men standing by their horses [at Knightsbridge Barracks] ready to start at a moment's notice, either for Windsor or for Kensington Palace ... None of the officers left the mess-room that night ... It must have been a wonderful scene, all these young men, with one topic, one name on their lips, waiting for orders ... Shortly Lord B. came in, stood in the middle of the room, and held up his hand amidst a dead silence. 'Gentleman' he said in a loud, clear voice, 'the King is dead. Let us drink to the new Sovereign - God save the Queen!' Loud and ringing cheers followed; again and again they rose and fell. No

one thought of the dear King, lying cold and stiff at Windsor; they only thought of the bright young life opening before them at Kensington, of the girl queen still sound asleep, though messengers were hurrying to tell her the great news.

'Gentlemen' again said the Colonel, 'all are to remain in the barracks till orders come from the War Office as to the destination of Her Majesty's Life Guards …'

Later, after escorting the Queen to Kensington Palace,

returning to the barracks, my father reported himself to Lord B., who had sat up, anxious to hear how all had gone off … Acting on Lord Melbourne's advice, [my father] went at once to the War Office, and resigned his commission. Lord B. and the other officers were much upset at his action, Lord B. saying prophetically 'You will live to regret it; no man at your time of life can give up his country and become a foreigner. The days will come when your heart will ache for the old corps, and you will long to be even a trooper amongst us all.'

(The author's father had decided on a career as a diplomat, and the widespread consequences of a new monarch's accession made this a suitable time for such a change of direction. In fact he went abroad with Ernest Augustus (1771-1851), duke of Cumberland, fifth son of George III, who succeeded on King William's death, in accordance with Salic law, as King Ernest I of Hanover.)

A.M.F. also records some years later that

Lord B., my father's old Colonel, was another visitor to Hanover, charged with an autograph letter from the Queen announcing her marriage with Prince Albert. He said the Prince took a great interest in the regiment, often going to watch them drill, and was taking lessons in the riding school in order to learn the seat of an Englishman on horseback. 'He is very quiet and silent' said Lord B., 'but has lots of pluck, for he is ready to mount any horse we put him on.' He had been once to the mess, and seemed astonished at the luxury of it, and the deep potations of wine in which the young officers indulged. Lord B. had to propose his health, and the Prince returned thanks in a neat and appropriate speech, though with a strong German accent, laughingly saying to Lord B. 'I shall speak better English when I have lived longer here.' …

The day after his arrival Lord B. was presented to King Ernest, and was not much pleased with the interview. His Majesty, who was in one of his bad humours, had put a lot of 'side on' as he expressed it, since he had become King: he was generally out of temper when he had news from the English Court. However, he recovered his temper the next day, asked Lord B. to dinner, and in most kind and gracious terms proposed the health of the young couple, and while his private band struck up the National air, the King remained standing all the time. 'I did it handsomely', he said to my father, whose turn it was to attend on him, 'I don't think the Queen would do the same for me.' He presented Lord B. with a handsome jar of Sèvres china, and would have decorated him with the Order of the Guelph, but he knew it was against the custom in England to wear foreign Orders without permission from the Sovereign.

Of Lord Melbourne Lord B. spoke in the warmest terms, saying he was the best Minister England had ever had. There was a strong cabal against him in London, many people fancying that he had too much influence with the Queen; but he always gave her the best advice on politics, the most fatherly guidance in anything connected with her domestic life, and she looked up to and listened to him as if he were her father. 'England is prosperous' said Lord B., 'and, as the Duke of Sussex told you, you were a fool to throw up all prospects and bury yourself here. People are soon forgotten when they leave the stage, and no manager takes an actor back again.' To which my father remarked that he was perfectly happy, and had no wish to return.

Lord B. left the following day for Berlin, as he wished to see the cavalry barracks there and ascertain if he could pick up any hints for his regiment. My father gave him a letter of introduction to Moltke, who was most useful and kind to him, taking him behind all the scenes. He was much struck with the discipline and steadiness of the Prussian cavalry soldiers, but wrote 'there is no soldier in physique, bearing and drill who can come up to our soldiers of the Life Guards.' He was devoted to his men and officers, and never quite forgave my father for 'deserting them' as he called it. He gave Moltke a warm invitation to come to London and visit our barracks, but the famous general did not care to cross the English Channel, and in his heart looked down on our army.

King Ernest asked my father many questions about Lord B.'s visit, and was curious to hear what the English Colonel had said of him, and, when he heard that Lord B. said 'he put too much side on', he laughed with the greatest good humour, and replied that he did not put on half as much side as many young Guardsmen: 'Your Colonel forgets that in England I was only a royal Duke, now I am a King of a powerful nation.'

The writer was incorrect in referring to 'Colonel' Henry at the time of his visit, for he had been promoted to Major-General on the accession of Queen Victoria, and was always known as 'General Henry' thereafter; also, of course, he did not succeed to the Beauchamp title until 1853. But in complete contrast to all the pettiness of High Society gossip is a letter received by Henry a few years previously, which evidently touched him so deeply that he preserved it amongst his private papers. It says much for his personality that one of his soldiers could gauge instinctively the right approach to adopt, and this letter is not without a few similar instances:

High Wycombe, 22nd Feb. 1826.

Dear Colonel,
I hope you will please to take it into consideration and grant me leave this time to be married for the young woman is one that will sute me very well and I should not like to be the death of her and I am almost sure that if we cannot be married that she will break her heart and I am afraid that will be the death of me or els drive me out of my mind to think that I have been the cause of anybody's death - and a married life is a thing that will keep a man from all bad company and from getting drunk and

absent - and you will find me all the better Soldier - therefore I trust to God that you will grant me this favour for the sake of the young woman and her Mother which are both almost broken-hearted about it and in so dowing you will very much oblige

Your humble servant, Solomon Frye, Corpl. 1st Life Guards.

Henry became Lieutenant-General in 1815 following Waterloo and a full General in 1854. He was Colonel of the 10th Hussars from 1816 to 1831, and of the 2nd Life Guards for the six months before his death in 1863.

Yet another glimpse of his character is given in a letter written to his grandson the seventh earl, by a close family friend: 'Your Grandfather, though of a kind heart, had a good deal of the Martinet in him, and his sons were somewhat rigidly brought up.'

Henry was his mother's favourite son, and it was probably due to her encouragement that he entered politics in 1816 as M.P. for Worcestershire. He held the seat until 1831, in which election he lost consequent upon a redrawing of boundaries creating a new constituency of West Worcestershire. His mother was extremely angry about his defeat and made no secret of her intention to spend at least £20,000 to see him re-elected (there was then no legislation against such expenditure). A stormy election followed only a year later, when his mother and her closest friends agreed that it was absolutely essential to have one person in charge of arrangements in the week leading up to and on the day of the actual election. That one person, they all agreed, was the bailiff, Jarvis Arnold, for no one but he knew all the electors on the Madresfield estates and was so well placed to secure their votes. This time Henry was elected and continued to hold the seat until he succeeded to the title on the death of his brother. During his 31 years as a Member he very rarely spoke in Parliament, but could always be relied on to take a safe, conventional stance when his vote was required.

Throughout Henry's life the army took first place, but he was far from being a tough, hardened soldier. In fact, as the correspondence arising from several family bereavements shows, he was on such occasions literally incapacitated by grief. The first event of this kind sets the tone for others.

Henry married in 1824 Lady Susan Caroline Eliot, daughter of the second Earl of St. Germans in Cornwall. In the following 11 years they had seven children, of whom only four survived. She died in 1835. Henry was in Derbyshire when he was informed of her illness, and he set off at once on horseback for St. Austell, where they were staying, riding through the night in an attempt to arrive before her death. He reached there an hour or so after she had passed away. Her housekeeper-cum-nurse, Eliza Marks, had kept a harrowing, hour by hour account of Lady Susan's illness, and to this she added a note of his arrival. Faced with the prospect of rearing the four young children, the soldier husband was distraught, but his wife had commended them to the care of her housekeeper and he was relieved to hand them over completely to so trusted a servant. Lady Susan also left him a last letter, which shows a picture of a devoted wife, but she was anxious—not only for the sake of the children but for his also—that he should in due course remarry. However, somewhat surprisingly for someone in his position and of his age—he was only 50—Henry remained a widower until his own death 28 years later. His reaction to his wife's death was almost hysterical outbursts of grief, when he asked only to be left alone to mourn, sometimes for quite prolonged periods.

Henry, a very practical man, had little sympathy with the religious controversies of the time, but he regarded himself as a staunch Church of England supporter. It was therefore rather surprising to find amongst his papers a short pencilled meditation on the *Anima Christi*. This is especially so as in his later years he was deeply concerned about the religious opinions of his second son Frederick, who, much involved in Church matters, maintained for some years an apparently ambivalent attitude towards Roman Catholics, rather like the Tower of Pisa's strong inclination without final capitulation; but eventually Henry came to trust that his son had no intention of quitting the church of his birth.

Although the children's grandmother, Countess Catherine Beauchamp, was still alive, she spent much of her time in London and Paris, and seems to have showed little interest in them. She occasionally spent short periods in the summer on her small estate, Spring Hill, near Broadway, but her real habitat was the city, preferably Paris or London. Her grandchildren were allowed to spend their summer holidays at Spring Hill, which became their favourite residence. Henry and his younger brother Edward also used it for shooting and hunting, but none of them visited Madresfield Court, where their estranged brother, John, the third earl, was living.

It was only a year before John's death that Henry and his younger daughter received an invitation to dine. This led to the healing of the rift in the family; Henry was acknowledged as the heir presumptive to the Madresfield estates and began to help in their management. Edward, the youngest brother, now also a General, bought himself a small property at Callow

Lady Susan Lygon

End, which he named St. Cloud in memory of one of the battles in which he had served, and here Henry and Georgiana frequently stayed in order to be within easy reach of the Court, but the first invitation to stay there overnight took some months to materialise.

By the time he succeeded to the title at the beginning of 1853, General Henry was in his 69th year, his elder daughter was dead, Henry his heir was an officer in the Life Guards, and his younger son, Frederick, was living in Oxford as a Fellow of All Souls' and absorbed in both academic and political life. His only constant companion was his younger daughter Georgiana, and with her he moved into Madresfield Court, with Miss Marks, the one-time nurse-cum-housekeeper, in charge of the domestic side. They brought some semblance of renewal to the Court, and General Henry, as he continued to be known, seemed content to settle down as a county landowner, largely retiring from public life.

The new occupants of the Court soon brought a changed atmosphere locally. The advent of three unmarried young people—Henry the heir, Frederick the scholar, and Georgiana the lively young lady who had been called 'the belle of the Regiment' at 16—brightened up Malvern's, not to say Worcestershire's, social life considerably, as the family became attached to their new home. Even the General was not quite safe from the attentions of a neighbouring landowner's daughter, who had set her sights on him long ago and now rejoiced in new possibilities. Sad to tell, these were never fulfilled.

General Henry also found a fresh interest. Hitherto his great passion had been horses and their breeding, especially for racing and hunting. Now he became enthralled with new methods of agriculture, and was the first to introduce mechanised farming to Worcestershire when he bought one of the first steam-powered tractors and drove it into Malvern to display it behind the then Beauchamp Hotel (now the Royal Arms) at the junction of Church Street with Graham Road. It was rented out to farmers on his estate for ploughing and reaping, at a very moderate charge. He also provided in his will for the building of three bridges over part of the back drive to the Court. This enabled him to give the local people the passage they required as a short cut to Powick and Callow End, and enabled them to avoid the toll house near the junction of Genetree Lane with the Newland road, whilst removing the intrusion of a public way into the most private part of the Court grounds.

He also provided, by a private Act of Parliament, for the public highway to be re-routed. At the time it followed, coming from Barnards Green, the present South Drive as far as the Home Farm, and so to the left to pass between the Court and the ancient church to join the road to the Old Hills. The new route took it past the present lychgate, (the boundary of the rector's glebe) past the end of the present drive at North Lodge and then joined the toll road to Worcester near the end of North End Lane, where eventually an oak tree was planted by General Henry in memory of the Battle of Waterloo. Unfortunately this was cut down by the County Council in the 1980s without consultation, and later the last Countess Beauchamp replaced it with another in memory of her husband, the eighth and last Earl Beauchamp; but it seems unlikely local people will ever forgive the County Council, for the Waterloo Oak was a treasured landmark.

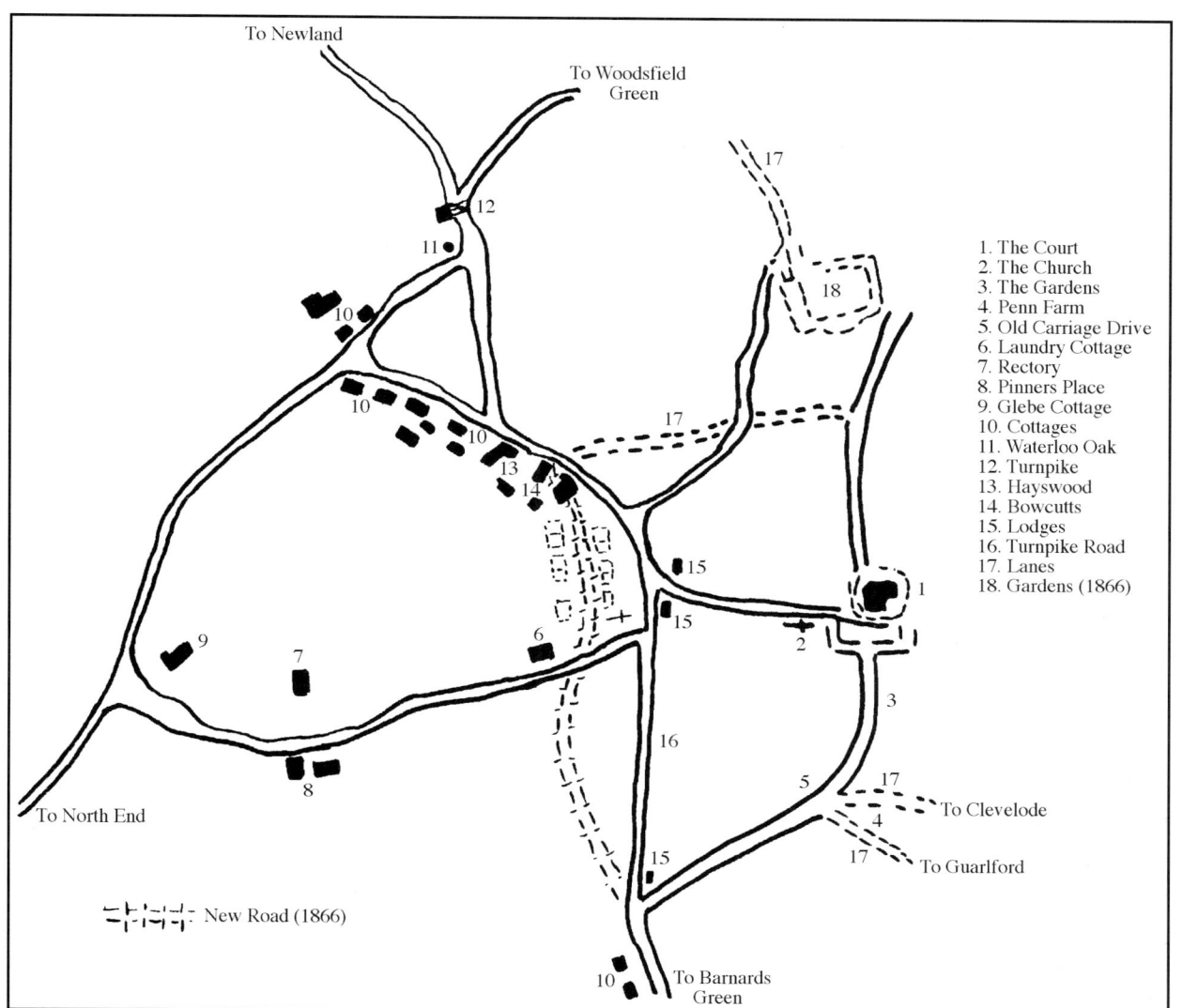

Madresfield c.1840 (not to scale)

General Henry also gave the village what it had never had—its own burial ground. He donated a piece of land known as Parsonage Close some distance away from the ancient church, for he had plans to build a new church though its site had not then been finally decided, but it seemed advisable to place the graveyard beside the new main road which would make for easy access. Until then, coffins had to be hauled either over the Old Hills to Powick or up the steep climb to Malvern Priory. Of course, as burial in consecrated ground was not mandatory, possibly some never made such a difficult journey. It is frequently impossible to trace the burials of earlier residents of the village.

The work on the new church was not far advanced when General Henry died in 1863. But the burial ground was ready; a new rector, appointed in 1853, had been in the parish only three weeks when his wife died and he ensured that the ground so long promised was consecrated at last, just in time for her funeral. General Henry was the first Lygon to be buried there; the later reburial of others is dealt with in chapter eleven.

Had it not been for the death of Lady Susan, General Henry's wife, at so early an age, we might never have known quite so much about a rather unexplored aspect of the early Oxford Movement, when the giants of the Tractarians were just beginning to emerge, and how already their teachings were reaching the nurseries of the influential families in England.

General Henry had placed his children in the care of Miss Eliza Marks who, although originally employed as housekeeper, had nursed Lady Susan in her last hours and who had become to a great extent her confidante. Eliza and her sister Susan had previously kept a small milliner's shop in Worcester, but had come to help Lady Susan as her family increased, at a time when the young mother lived principally in Cornwall but also had a home in London. Shortly after Lady Susan's death, when the bereaved family returned to London with their father, Miss Eliza assumed authority as the children's governess, and one or two small changes she introduced are highly significant. She herself became Miss Marks, and not the hitherto familiar 'Markey', her sister, no longer a nursery nurse, became Miss Susan and her deputy, whilst her brother was drawn in as the children's drawing master. Since none of these three spoke French, a teacher had to be employed but her influence was confined to a few hours a week. Of Lady Susan's four surviving children, the eldest, eleven-year-old Felicia, dropped her nicknames of Flizzy and 'Licia and became Miss Lygon to all but her siblings, who were instructed to address her as 'Sister'. 'Master Henry' and 'Master Frederick' probably enjoyed their new dignity, but little Georgiana, just three, whose father could refuse her nothing, was allowed to remain Georgy for the present—a fatal lapse of discipline, for she chose to retain the abbreviation for the rest of her life.

Lady Susan could have had no inkling of the fate that was waiting for her children, for although her own mother died whilst she was very young, her father was subsequently married and widowed on three further occasions, so that she and her sisters and one brother had three stepmothers in fairly quick succession, and these seem to have been willingly accepted. Perhaps the father's tact was responsible, for there is still preserved the letter in which he announced to his young daughters the first remarriage when they were living temporarily with an old family friend, the Countess of Ely:

> November 2, 1808.
> My dearest little Girls, I have something to tell you that will give you great pleasure indeed. I know that you would like very much to live always with me in the same house and be constantly with me as you used to be ... I should like it quite as much as you do, but I have denied myself the pleasure of seeing your little merry faces all day long, because I thought it better for you and more for your good to live with Lady Ely who was so fond of you. Little Girls who have had the misfortune that you have had to be deprived of their Mama cannot be so well brought up by their Papa who has so much to do and is fully employed, as they can by some kind friend like Lady Ely, who puts herself as much as can be in the place of their dear Mama - When it pleased God Almighty to take your dear Mama into heaven ... she talked a great deal about what ... would be best to supply her place. She then earnestly desired me to find a young Lady whom I could love, and who would love you all and cherish and protect you ... and

having found such a person your Mama's last signified wish to me was that I should make her my wife, and consequently your mother.

I have now found this second Mama, for you my dearest Girls. She will love you and talk to you and treat you as her little friends ... we shall again live all together you will see her making me happy and for that cause be inclined to love her the more ...

Lady Ely will answer any questions you wish to ask on the subject of this Letter.

Lord St. Germans certainly knew the right approach to take with his daughters, for each stepmother in her turn was loyally accepted, and her relations in each case remained on affectionate terms with the St. Germans' family during the lifetime of the three girls, so that eventually Susan's children inherited a cluster of distant but valued connections. But the Eliots of St. Germans remained closest to the Lygons of Madresfield, whose mother had been replaced by so strict a governess.

After Lady Susan's funeral, the Earl of St. Germans took his other two daughters, Lady Caroline and Lady Charlotte, to stay on the Continent for some months. They were all earnest Evangelical Christians, and Lady Caroline, in particular, was concerned for the religious upbringing of the children. Perhaps to ensure that Miss Marks was continuing the good work started by Lady Susan, Lady Caroline requested that Felicia should send her a written account of her progress and behaviour once a fortnight. So there still exists the child's 'journal' kept over a period of approximately three months.

Felicia was an articulate child, her spelling impeccable and her handwriting usually clear and firm, except when, as happened eventually, it was smudged with tears. Somehow

Madresfield Court in 1861

Madresfield Court in 1861

Miss Marks became interested in the religious turmoil of the time. At least once, more usually twice, sometimes three times every Sunday, she took the children to church. Occasionally this was to their local parish church, St. Peter's, Eaton Square, but she also explored other, more esoteric places. There were a dozen 'tin chapels' springing up, but she became quite attached to the first St. Margaret's at Oxford Circus probably before even Butterfield, the great Victorian church architect, had heard of it, and then there was St. Alban's at Holborn Circus and many others.

But Sundays were not nearly enough for her religious observance. She ordered Felicia to examine her conscience each night and to write the result in her journal for her aunt's edification. This requirement put poor Felicia in something of a quandary, for most of the 'sins' she had to record concerned feelings of resentment for Miss Marks and her conduct. However, one suspects that she eventually resolved this dilemma quite cleverly, by closely examining the roots of her resentment and so conveying something of her real difficulties to her beloved Aunt Caro. For instance, if Miss Marks forbade her to do something for which her father had already given permission, she could describe her bitter disappointment quite fully and then go on to explain how guilty she felt because she knew dear Miss Marks was only disciplining her for her soul's good. Her journal was always enclosed with a report from Miss Marks, in which that lady detailed her trials with the children and her constant endeavours to correct their innate tendencies to evil.

The Lygon children's father was unlike the Eliots'. General Henry was a soldier toughened, at least outwardly, by war, who despite having been close to death on more than one occasion confined his religious practices to one Sunday a month at most. However, his much-loved wife had had absolute confidence, apparently, in Eliza Marks'

Madresfield Court in 1861

opinions on religious matters. She could no doubt be trusted to inculcate desirable principles. Lord St. Germans had not remarried after the death of his fourth wife a few years previously; the redoubtable Countess Catherine Beauchamp spent most winters in Paris, and even when she visited London seemed content to leave the upbringing of her numerous grandchildren to others. Sometimes, when she was in London, she might summon them to a meeting, which they would attend with trepidation; or Aunt Lady Louisa might pay a brief visit to Brook Street to inspect them on her behalf; only one cousin, Charles Pakenham, son of their young Aunt Catherine, the widowed Countess of Longford, came occasionally within Miss Marks' orbit, and she was to affect him also in the years to come.

Part of Miss Marks' regime associated with Felicia's journal was that the child was obliged to write a resumé of every sermon she heard, perhaps to reassure Aunt Caroline they were not being led astray as much as for the child's own edification; there is frequently evidence of the really quite orthodox teaching of some of the more famous preachers, whose chief offence was often their love of ritual.

Yet even at this very early stage there is one quotation from Felicia's letters which sounds a warning note. As the eldest child of a general once so severely wounded, Felicia struggled to show herself determined to overcome any physical weakness. She was on one occasion ridiculed at the advanced age of nearly 11 for 'crying like a baby, for Miss Marks thinks that it is very fortunate that I have a tooth out now and then that I may know what a little pain is and may gain a little fortitude.' That encouragement to stoicism may well have had a disastrous effect on both Felicia and her sister Georgy in their adult lives.

The journal seems to have been discontinued after Lady Caroline returned to England in the autumn, but not long afterwards the two boys were sent away to school at

Eton, and within a couple of years Felicia had taken on the task of ensuring that the duty of letter-writing was not neglected; throughout their teens she wrote to them regularly, scolding them like a loving mother when necessary, nor did the pattern change when Henry progressed to Oxford.

But then, in 1845, Felicia fell in love. She was 20, a pretty, lively girl; a number of desirable suitors had already noticed her, but she chose a penniless young man, Charles Cavendish, grandson of the Duke of Devonshire, who was seeking ordination as a Church of England clergyman. One feels that it was she who chose him; her father was unenthusiastic, but, perhaps to balance his rather stern treatment of his two sons, he was inclined to indulge his girls, as he called them. He gave his consent, but then came a tussle over the marriage settlement, for the young man's father, General Charles Cavendish, was not rich and proved very reluctant to help the young couple set up house. He had already promised his son the living of Little Stamford in Lincolnshire, but this was very slow to materialise, as were also the promised pony and trap. However, Felicia was to receive under the will of her grandfather the first Earl Beauchamp an amount of £60,000 on marriage.

The wedding took place in September 1847. There are two contrasting accounts of it in letters to the younger brother Frederick: from Felicia recounting how although very nervous she had behaved with complete composure, and the other from Georgy describing Felicia's great agitation and how on entering the church she had to be given a chair so that she could recover herself before proceeding up the aisle. The newly-weds spent their honeymoon in a house lent by the Cavendishes on the edge of Hyde Park, while they waited for confirmation that Charles would be given the living in Lincolnshire. At last this came, and he was ordained as a priest at the end of December.

At Little Stamford the rectory found no favour in Felicia's eyes. She immediately decided that its existing orientation must be changed, and work started on converting the back entrance to be a quite imposing front, and similarly inside. She also found herself the necessary staff, but very soon running into difficulties with the cook she appealed to Miss Marks to come and advise her. It was not only the house she reorganised. The little church was of course quite plain and unadorned. Felicia decided the altar must have flowers, and various other embellishments, which her husband, who had not had her experience of the new High Church thinking, watched with something approaching dismay, frightened as to the possible reaction of his parishioners. She also insisted not only on a Sunday morning service, but also one for children in the afternoon, followed by Evensong, and twice-weekly celebrations of Holy Communion. Her cook and housemaid were expected to attend most of these, although the groom seems to have been let off with only one service on Sundays. It is hardly surprising that her husband called her his High Priestess.

Her letters show how happy she was and how she delighted in her new work, above all in her duties as organist, for she was very musical and had soon recruited and begun to train a choir. And then, as July passed into August, there is a subtle change which should have rung a warning bell. Twice, letters which she had started to Frederick are completed by her husband because she is too tired to finish them. Until now she had driven herself as well as others unmercifully—one can always hear in the background Miss Marks' stern dictum about enduring a little pain. Then, in her last letter to Frederick she tells him that before she writes again she will have, God willing, a little nephew or niece for him to love. Meanwhile, next Saturday being her first wedding anniversary, she has resolved to give the cook and housemaid, and the groom, a holiday and she will cook dinner for them—roast beef and plum pudding.

But early on that Saturday morning she went into labour, late that night gave birth to a stillborn daughter, and as Sunday dawned she died.

The family reacted according to their characters in predictable fashion. Her brother Henry was with his regiment, and there was no question of his asking for leave to attend her funeral. Frederick was due to go up to Oxford on the Monday, and his father insisted he did so. Georgiana remained in London, for young ladies did not often attend funerals. Only her father, General Henry, and the uncle who was adored by all the children, General Edward, were present to represent the Lygons.

Georgiana, a merry 16-year-old who had always been her father's favourite and to whom he rarely refused anything, now found herself bombarded from all sides on her duty to devote herself in future to her father. He was indeed a tragic figure, sitting day after day weeping by the fire and joined by his widowed son-in-law, who had taken rooms nearby in order to be close to Felicia's relations. But at last the doctor took firm action. He ordered that Charles Cavendish should ration his visits, as he was only daily renewing the General's distress, and the task of dissuading Charles was laid on Miss Marks, who evidently carried it out successfully. Charles later lost touch with the family; he remarried twice, but had only an adopted daughter, and finally he became a Roman Catholic.

Georgy developed her talent for music in a somewhat surprising way. She was, of course, the organist of Madresfield Church and choirmistress, fiercely resentful of anyone who took over her duties if she was away. But the concertina had recently been invented and was very fashionable. She learned to play this instrument in London, and on at least one occasion appeared on stage with a fashionable concertina group. Eventually she married the eldest son of the Earl of Raglan, he who famously fought in the Crimean War and is credited with responsibility for the charge of the Light Brigade. On that occasion he had been riding a magnificent black horse known as Shadrach. Later his son brought the horse to Worcestershire and hunted him on several occasions. On the last he rode the horse probably excessively, for at the end of the day it failed a jump and had to be put down at once. It was later honoured with a grave and a plaque on the front drive to Madresfield Court.

It was also whilst they were hunting that a close friend noticed that Georgy, an enthusiastic horsewoman, was having some difficulty, and subsequent examination revealed that she had in fact some months before lost the sight of one eye, but would not speak about it because of their strict upbringing never to complain.

When she left Madresfield on her marriage, she took with her their old nurse, Miss Susan Marks, who had come to the Lygons at the time of her birth. Miss Susan died in June 1864, Georgy (in childbirth) on 30 September, 1865, and Miss Marks on 17 December in the same year.

Charles Reginald Pakenham

Charles Pakenham—who was known as 'Charlie P.' to distinguish him from Felicia's husband 'Charlie C.'—was only a couple of years older than Felicia, and perhaps it was because of this that of all the cousins he seems to have been affected most by Miss Marks and the religious interest she had stimulated in her charges. His mother was Catherine, that daughter of the first earl whose wedding to the second Earl of Longford had had to be postponed because of her father's unexpected death. Married to a man twice her age, she was left a widow 20 years later with eight sons and three daughters, in somewhat straitened circumstances.

Her two elder sons were already at Sandhurst; Charles, the third, was also destined for a military career. General Edward immediately made him his protégé and from then on Charles' home was with the General either at Spring Hill or in his Brook Street house in London. He was sent to Sandhurst three months before his 14th birthday, and appeared to have a promising military future ahead of him—two uncles well respected in Army circles might have been considered a guarantee of that—but there was a hint of misfortune in that he was also a nephew of Wellington's wife and therefore related to the despised Pakenhams, the late Lord Longford's sister being the unhappy Duchess of Wellington. (The Duchess apparently incurred her husband's unrelenting antipathy when she used part of her housekeeping allowance to subsidise her rather spendthrift brother's expenditure, but the Duke's enduring bitterness seems to have been entirely disproportionate.)

After four years at Sandhurst, Charles was gazetted to the 72nd Regiment. This regiment being at the time in the West Indies, he had to join it there, but after only a few weeks they returned home. In due course, he found himself a captain in the 1st Battalion of Grenadier Guards as aide-de-camp to the Inspector-General of Cavalry, his uncle General Edward, on 20 October, 1846. It is interesting that this date, only a few days after Felicia's wedding, is the starting point for a small book of quotations kept by Charles from various authors over a very wide range indeed, all quoted in their original languages—English, German, French, Italian, Spanish—on a number of religious themes. His linguistic skill is not surprising, for he and his cousins were accustomed to correspond in several European languages, usually to frustrate Miss Marks' curiosity. But the subjects which he was evidently studying indicate how his mind had turned away from military matters, and towards those which he would have been discussing with Felicia and her brother Frederick, both of whom were strongly attracted to the new Anglo-Catholicism which was disturbing the Church of England. He must have followed with considerable interest Felicia's brave attempts to introduce some rituals into the parish church at Little Stamford.

But when in 1850 Charles decided to become a Roman Catholic, it came as a great shock to his uncles, the two generals, to whom it seemed inconceivable that a Lygon would take such a step. Worse was to come. Less than a year later he entered the novitiate of the Passionist Order at Broadway, having sold his commission in the Guards together with some other possessions and given the money to charity. General Edward was deeply upset, but he, along with the others at Madresfield Court, refused to disown Charles, as his own family the Pakenhams did even to the extent of deleting his name from the

Longford records in *Debrett*. When after a year or two, Charles' health gave away under the strict regime, General Edward disregarded all Passionist austerities and sent Madresfield grapes and grouse to his nephew. Sadly, he possibly never tasted these, for they were shared amongst the novitiate. He recovered, and duly progressed in the novitiate, so that when local Catholic schools were opened in Broadway with as much pomp and ceremony as could be managed, it was he who was chosen to carry the cross at the head of the procession. He was of course the obvious choice for such a duty, being like all his family over six feet tall, and with the impeccable carriage of an ex-Guardsman, but Worcestershire did not so easily forgive his defection; the local paper commented that 'The Honourable Charles Reginald Pakenham, who has lately become a lay brother among the Passionists, degraded himself by carrying the cross.'

Charles later changed his name to Paul Mary, and less than four years after his conversion was ordained priest. He went to study in Rome, but after a few months was recalled to England and then sent to found the first house of his order in Ireland, known to generations of Dubliners ever since as Mount Argus. He had been born in Dublin, and regarded himself as 'an Irishman through and through', to quote a close friend. He undertook the task of forming his small group of brothers into true representatives of their order, and was unremitting in his insistence upon its austerities; yet he also became extremely popular with the local people. But he was like a blazing fire which burnt itself out too quickly. He had come to Dublin in the summer of 1856, and he died on 1 March, 1857. He was mourned by the city as a saint, and on the day of his funeral all traffic was brought to a halt. There was talk of starting a Cause for his beatification, but nothing came of it, perhaps because it was well-known where his political sympathies lay. He came from a family of the 'ascendancy' in Ireland, which had always been antagonistic to the nationalist cause; living with his uncle General Edward he had known great wealth, yet he embraced the ideal of Poverty with more fervour than some of his Passionist colleagues; but he was well-read in Irish history, had known the terrible effects of the Famine; he had seen how often the English treated their horses better than their Irish employees. All this was summed up in one remark he made during his last illness, when, asked to relent the sternness in his attitude vis-a-vis the English, he replied simply 'Ireland has nothing to thank England for'. It was definitely not the sort of comment guaranteed to endorse one's suitability for sainthood, though one must admire its honesty. But there is a somewhat surprising sequel to his story.

Thirty-seven years after his death, it was decided to build a new chapel at Mount Argus. This necessitated a new cemetery and the removal of remains from the original burial place. For some reason the coffin of Fr. Paul Mary, born Charles Pakenham, was opened, 'and the body then found perfectly intact and incorrupt, and the face wore a most lifelike expression as of one who lay in a peaceful slumber' as his official biographer expressed it. These were signs regarded in ancient times as significant of exceptional holiness. There were a considerable number of witnesses.

There is another example in Dublin of corpses remaining intact without any attempt at preservation such as the Egyptians used in mummification: H.V. Morton gives a vivid account of the scores of bodies preserved in the vault of St. Michan's (Anglican) Church in Dublin, all of whom died within the last 900 years, including at least one Crusader, which have never decayed and whose flesh now resembles black leather. The phenomenon is said to be due to the air having been chemically impregnated by the remains of an oak forest which stood there in ancient times. Perhaps there was some similar agent in the soil at Mount Argus. However, anyone who has seen the vaults at St. Michan's is likely to share Morton's horror at the spectacle of innumerable bodies, preserved indefinitely, provided they are not exposed to moisture. It is not a pleasant sight and would not encourage any viewer to regard it as a sign of sanctity. It is unlikely that a Passionist would have been buried in any but the simplest and cheapest of coffins, so that there was no protection in that respect.

Whatever the reason for this unaided preservation, Charles Pakenham deserves to be remembered for the high ideals to which he paid much more than lip service, and for which he sacrificed everything, inspired by Felicia Lygon and Eliza Marks.

CHAPTER NINE
Henry, Fifth Earl Beauchamp (1829-1866)

Henry, the eldest son of General Henry, was born on 13 February 1829 in London. He was the first Lygon to be sent to Eton for his education; until then, he had come under the rule of Miss Marks in the nursery. She, no doubt suitably impressed that her young charge might well become the earl one day since his elder uncle had no children and the next in line was unmarried, was as strict with him as she dared, but not quite so demanding as with his siblings. Henry was apparently a delicate child and, at least in his sister Felicia's opinion, quite capable of feeling unwell to suit his immediate preferences. This was evidenced by 'the pill' which he had to take frequently, but he timed the taking of the pill very carefully, so that it could sometimes be the reason for missing church, and as all the children resented their enforced regular attendance Henry could always gain their sympathy when needed.

He was, however, seized very early in his life by a passion to be a soldier like his father, and Miss Marks could use this weapon against him; at first she urged obedience and duty, later she pointed out that no army would accept an unfit recruit. So for most of his childhood the battle went on, but what remained with Henry for life was a sense of lack of sympathy, though in fact his siblings were extremely patient with him. Leaving Eton, he was sent abroad with a tutor to Switzerland to perfect his French and Italian. When his elder sister Felicia died, letters exchanged between father and son at the time reveal two small but significant details—his father refers to Felicia not now by the childhood names of Flizzy and 'Licia which he had continued to use despite Miss Marks, but calls her Mrs Cavendish; perhaps he had disapproved of her marriage too much to forgive her—and in reply Henry's only comment is that he is glad he was not at her funeral since General Cavendish (her father-in-law) was present.

He had returned to England as soon as his father secured a commission for him in the Life Guards and commenced his military career in May, 1848, with bright prospects. He soon became a typical officer of his day, developing a passion for horses—he spent much of his time training other officers and men alike to become expert horsemen—and, when he could get leave, which was surprisingly often, in travelling. But as soon as his father became Earl Beauchamp in 1852, the new Viscount Elmley, as Henry became, sold his commission and spent a prolonged period abroad, undertaking the Grand Tour, visiting, in addition to France, Italy, and Germany, St. Petersburg, Moscow and Turkey. He followed this in 1853 with a visit to America, Cuba and Canada.

He was strictly conscientious about writing to his father at least every fortnight, and so one opens his bundles of letters with high hopes of finding interesting glimpses of his reaction to all the foreign lands. But unfortunately Henry only rarely obliges in this respect. Most of his letters consist of complaints that his father and his siblings do not write to him, or fail to tell him the most recent gossip when they do put pen to paper. The longest description of anything he has seen comes from Moscow (or, as he insists on calling it, Mus-cow) in August, 1852:

> Mus-cow is a very fine town and there is a good deal to see here. In going over the treasury, Library and Palace this morning, I wished several times that Gen'l Edward [his uncle] could have been with me; the collection of curiosities, and all sorts of both ancient and more modern articles of all description is most wonderful. The magnificence of the Kremlin is past all belief, the quantity of Marble, Malachite, diamonds, and precious stones makes one fancy that it is fairy land rather than anything real.

But then he recollects that he is an Englishman and reverts to the weather:

> The weather at St Petersburg was nothing more than what one should call fine summer weather, not nearly so hot as it was in London ...

Wherever he went Henry made a point of staying with the local military if possible, and if not, at least sharing in the officers' mess. Now and again he may comment briefly on their methods of training or their equipment, but all his letters have one constantly recurring complaint: he has had no letters from home, or, if they do arrive, they have had none of the Society gossip in which he delighted. Occasionally he may ask his sister if Lady X is engaged yet, or whether Miss Y has caught her quarry, although he himself seems never to have formed any long-term attachment. Whilst she was still alive, his sister Felicia could scold him freely, but his attitude to his younger sister Georgy was one of great condescension, and one sympathises with her failure to be a frequent correspondent, good-natured though she was. In his letters to his father, he occasionally displays a dutiful interest in politics and public affairs, as befitted his position as heir apparent.

In 1853 he kept a journal when he visited America and Canada in the autumn, but the entries are laconic in the extreme; usually merely a note of places visited, people encountered, and his expenses. He travelled with a friend, Gerard Noel, and their valets. The voyage from Liverpool took him 9 days and 18 hours to New York, where he went to the theatre and a cricket match. Then he went on to Boston and after a few short outings pressed on to Canada, visiting Quebec, Montreal and Niagara. He then returned to New York and took a five day voyage to Cuba.

His first letter to his father after his arrival in Boston is typical:

> My dear Father - I suppose you will be expecting a letter from me about this time, so in order not to disappoint you I send you a few lines, though I have little to tell you

as we are not yet very far advanced in this little country. We had a splendid passage across the Atlantic as good as ever was known. I was only ill once and that as much from eating and smoking as from the sea. We had but a scrubby lot of passengers on board and no one worth mentioning except Madame Fiorentini who we tried to get to sing but we did not succeed.

We staid at New York 3 or 4 days, & then went to Newport which is a watering place (a sort of Cheltenham), about 70 miles off, we took letters of introduction with us and went into the thick of the gay world. After staying there 4 days we came on here and we have already seen a great deal of this place which we leave on Tuesday the 6th and taking the White mountains on our way we go to Montreal and after going to Quebec we shall proceed up the St Lawrence river and across Lake Ontario to Niagara and from there back to New York. The Steamers for America leave Liverpool every Saturday and Wednesday, so that a letter posted in London on a Tuesday or Friday evening reached New York in 10 days. I expect to be at New York on the 28th of this month so that if you will write me a line on receiving this letter directed to the 'Clarendon Hotel' 'New York' I shall be pretty sure to get it. We have Gerard Noel and Hamilton still with us so that we are a very jolly party, and we are likely to keep together so some time longer. ... The weather here is most superb, and without suffocating one is very hot.

I should like to hear what is going on 'chez vous' ... Ask Georgy and Freddy to write. I will write again from New York. Yrs. Henry.

When he next wrote their party had been joined by another two Englishmen and they had almost finished their look at Canada. The main event of recent weeks had been an Agricultural Show where fortunately the cattle on the whole met with his approval although

> the horses did not strike me as anything very superior ... There never was a greater mistake than supposing the American newspapers good, they are all cheap and trashy, a good sensible article is unknown in any of them and they are quite useless as far as intelligence is concerned and only serve to arouse the worst feelings of the people. The American hotels I consider all "humbug", nothing but show, all flash, and to anyone who has an Englishman's idea of comfort almost unbearable. The system of chewing in this country is something too odious, and I do not exaggerate at all when I say that it alone would prevent any Lady among such a filthy society but no! pull up, I could go on for an hour in this strain ...

From Canada he returned to New York and subsequently visited Cuba and Mexico. In Havana the weather was so hot as to be scarcely bearable but 'we were lucky enough to come in for a bull fight which has been one of my great desires to see for a long time past & I must say I am disappointed with this Spanish national pastime. I think it not only cruel but cold blooded and cowardly work.' He occupied himself most days with short, level drives, except one day he took a train to Metonyms; *en route* two carriages ran off the line so that he was considerably delayed. Returning via Santa Cruz they ran into a hurricane, and later got badly stuck in mud. This letter was dated 30 October but he adds that he hopes to be home by 28 December 'when I shall expect the fatted calf to be slain - though I shall not have to ask forgiveness for riotous living.'

When he visited Mexico the pattern was the same. But there was at the time considerable unrest in Latin America, and he had courage in venturing into the area just then. Next he went on to Guadeloupe and New Orleans where he 'saw New Orleans life' after dinner. He returned via Oregon and West Point to Atlanta. A few days later he went to Richmond where he saw the State House and the assembly of Senators, and so on to Washington. Here he 'went to the Smithsonian Museum ... the Capitol - paid a visit to the President.' He omits the President's name but it must have been Franklyn Pierce, who had recently become the fourteenth President since America had gained independence 70 years previously. Next he retraced his steps to New York and Boston, from where he sailed on 21 December for England, reaching Liverpool on 3 January, 1854, after a rough crossing which delayed his arrival.

It seems doubtful if Henry could ever be accused of riotous living. Throughout all his travels he stayed when possible with the local military, apparently being warmly welcomed by officers' messes wherever he went. Otherwise he stayed at hotels, which seldom met his standards, or with local hostelries, which he frequently suspected of having no object except to rob him. He kept a meticulous record of his expenses, which apart from travelling and accommodation show considerable expenditure on his clothing, about which he was very particular.

From the spring of 1853 until he succeeded his father, Henry served as M.P. for Worcestershire. He took a keen interest in overseeing purchases of land, and in the breeding of horses. He was also a very keen follower of

Henry, Fifth Earl Beauchamp

the hunt. He made only one more significant journey overseas, when he spent the last few months of 1862 visiting Algiers and Egypt partly in the pursuit of better health, but his letters continued to be disappointing in their content. It is frustrating for instance to read that 'I arrived here [Cairo] this morning as far up the Nile as Thebes' and then discover that for the rest of the letter he goes on to discuss the latest purchase of a farm adjoining the Madresfield Estate.

Succeeding his father as fifth Earl Beauchamp in September, 1863, Henry's tenure of the properties was marked from its beginning by ill-health. In 1864 he went to live in Brighton, in the hope that sea air would be beneficial, and as a result his brother Frederick had to take over the day to day management of the estates. It was a difficult duty which the younger man fulfilled conscientiously and with great tact, but the letters give little information. There had been some discussion between the brothers as to the rebuilding of parts of Madresfield Court and also the provision of a new church, but little progress had been made when Henry died on 4 March, 1866. He was buried in the 'new' churchyard at Madresfield, and the tenants and employees had to face yet once more considerable changes as the fresh thinking of another capable owner impinged on their lives.

The Saga of Madresfield Churches

Like his father, Henry had inherited the problem of providing a suitable church for Madresfield. The little 12th century building bequeathed by Anne Beauchamp had come to the end of its days, and for a number of years since their inheritance of the Jennens money the family had been planning to provide a new one, but all that had materialised had been the building of the mausoleum—a small parallelogram on the north side of the old chapel which has been variously described as a vault, a chapel or a mausoleum. The first and second earls had been buried here, followed in due course by four other members of the family.

The third earl, John Reginald Pindar, made no alterations to the ancient church, but instead decided to provide a larger place of worship at Madresfield. The tiny old church was therefore taken down in 1852, and a new one erected to a design by Augustus Pugin, one of the foremost architects of his day who had been largely responsible for the design of the interior of the Houses of Parliament.

Madresfield Church, looking at the east end

This second church is described as 'a parallelogram, with two projections on the north side, one of which contained seats for the family at the Court, the other the family vault, to which the old Norman doorway formed the entrance.' The jambs and tympanum of the 12th century entrance were thus preserved for a few more years, but now only the tympanum remains, built into the base of the cross erected in memory of the sixth earl, which stands on the site of the old church in the private grounds.

There are few pictures of the second church, but one attractive watercolour in the Court shows the congregation arriving on Sunday morning. A tall figure, presumably Lord Beauchamp, stands close to the porch to welcome them; two couples, perhaps guests, are approaching from the Court's front entrance; but coming from the opposite direction, having evidently left the Court by its back door, are the household staff: first half-a-dozen male servants, then the female—14 women all dressed alike in white bonnets, blue cloaks and red dresses, followed by a tall, commanding figure in deepest clerical black, who must be the redoubtable Mr. Munn, rector of the parish for almost 50 years from 1832. Significantly, the foreground of the picture, between the church and the land now attached to Home Farm, appears to be distinctly marshy, even having in one place a small wooden bridge and handrail.

With that picture in mind, it becomes easier to understand the fate that lay in wait for Pugin's church. It looked quite impressive, but of all the defects which any church might have, it had the most inappropriate. It not only lacked a sure foundation but had none at all, 'being built absolutely on the surface', according to Mr. Munn. This may have been due to the fact that it had been 'somewhat hastily reconstructed', as years later Frederick, the sixth earl, explained.

Though the reason for haste is not certainly known, it may be that John, the third earl, was anxious to see completion of his project, but he died in London in January, 1853. By his own wish he was buried beside his first wife in London (see p.52), perhaps this request was because of the current discussion about a new building for Madresfield. The commissioning of Pugin in 1851 and the commencement of work early in 1852 coincided with the reconciliation of the third earl with his brothers after their long alienation.

The Cross in the grounds that marks the site of the earlier church. The base contains the tympanum of the 12th-century entrance. The grave to the left is that of William, Eighth Earl Beauchamp

Looking through the screen to the altar, Madresfield Church

Another contributory factor to this omission of a foundation may have been Pugin's own tragic circumstances. Whilst it was Augustus Pugin whom the third earl commissioned to build the church, Augustus became insane in 1851 and died in 1852. His son, Edward, then only 17 years of age, inherited the practice. It fell to General Henry upon his succession to go ahead with the project, and he decided to divert the existing road from Barnards Green to Newland to its present route, so that instead of passing close to the Court it would lie considerably to the south-west, thereby giving the family greater privacy, an undertaking for which a private Act of Parliament was required and duly obtained. The building was soon completed, but by 1864, less than a year after General Henry's own death, the walls had settled and cracked to such an extent that the building was declared unsafe, only 12 years from commencement of its building.

The old church had been demolished; the new one was unsafe; so whilst the position was being considered and remedied, the services took place in the village school which had not long been built as a memorial to the third earl. It was eventually agreed to place church No. 3 opposite the school, on the new main road, on a large plot of land which General Henry had promised to the village as a burying-ground, and which had been consecrated as such in 1857.

So it fell to Henry, as fifth Earl Beauchamp, to find another architect. His choice fell upon another well-known architect, Frederick Preedy, to design the building. The builders went ahead slowly, making sure that this time the church did have solid foundations, but Henry never saw his new church, for he died more than two years before its completion.

There was then another element in the delay—Frederick the sixth earl's keen interest in architecture. As the third earl had provided the necessary finance for Pugin's church, so the fifth had provided Preedy's, which was to be similar in size to its predecessors; however, Frederick slightly enlarged it and added the tower, spire, bells and screen at his own expense.

As much as possible from the two previous churches was used in the construction of the third; for instance, the chancel roof is the entire roof of Pugin's unstable structure, compressed into a much smaller space, and the piscina in the vestry is an 18th-century baptismal font from the first church. The East window, part of the reredos, and the West window were all in Pugin's church. Whilst Preedy's church was being built, services were held in a temporary structure on the site (then included in the rector's glebe) of the present school. The well in the churchyard is said to have been sunk for the use of the workmen, although this seems somewhat unnecessary since the village, small as it was, had not only a plethora of wells but a choice of hard water at one end and soft at the other.

The new building was consecrated on 10 November, 1867, Frederick's 37th birthday, with a very full programme of services, including a confirmation, almost as though he was endeavouring to make amends for all the delays in providing a suitable church, and further services on the following Tuesday. The collections totalled £200, a very large amount at that time, and in addition and perhaps understandably the earl gave £100 to Worcester Royal Infirmary as a thankoffering that there had been so few accidents during the various building works carried out in Madresfield over recent years.

The newspapers of the time indulge in eulogies about the church. Only one—the *Worcester Herald*—did not feel obliged to be blindly uncritical:

> We may congratulate all parties in raising one of the most handsome and substantial churches (for its comparatively small size) in the diocese. We have qualified the word 'small' inasmuch as the structure, thought not accommodating 200 people, is sufficiently large to hold the entire parishioners, even if one and all turned out unanimously on any given day and went en masse to the sanctuary ... The chanting was antiphonal and the hymn 'Jerusalem the golden' was sung, but the musical part of the service was done far too rapidly to be devotional. There is a line to be drawn between the wretched droning which prevailed some years ago and the hurried scrambling now prevalent among so many of our church choirs ... The bells are by Messrs Taylor of Loughborough. The first and tenor bells are not satisfactory to our organ of tune, but a better authority than we has pronounced otherwise ...

The report concludes '150 clergy and gentry took lunch at the Court. We have to thank the Rector, Rev. G.S. Munn, for his courtesy and kind hospitality to the gentlemen of the press.' Perhaps if the reporter had lunched at the Court his report might have been more favourable.

Yet despite the reluctance of the parishioners to accept any responsibility for the maintenance and upkeep of the church for many years to come, it was from the consecration of the new building that Madresfield began to have, in the accepted sense, a parish church. The impact on Frederick the sixth earl of this removal of the centre of Madresfield's place of worship from its close proximity to the Court, which it had served as chapel for so many centuries, is perhaps indicated by the fact that at this time two rooms at the Court were converted into a private chapel and first used for services from Advent Sunday, 1866, when Frederick's close friend from Oxford, by now Canon H.P. Liddon of St. Paul's Cathedral, celebrated the Eucharist for the first time—and when Frederick's decision to marry was taken.

CHAPTER TEN
Frederick, Sixth Earl Beauchamp (1830-1891)

Frederick was the second son of General Henry Lygon and Lady Susan Eliot. Educated at Eton, he showed very early the temperament of a scholar, demonstrated in his strong attachment to books, especially those of an antiquarian nature, and to music. In both cases he had a very decided preference for examples of a religious nature. There was clear evidence of this towards the end of his time at Eton, just before he went up to Oxford, when a friend wrote asking him for a suggestion for a present to a mutual acquaintance who was about to be ordained; he was considering a Prayer Book but uncertain of what edition. Frederick, who had already, as befitted a Lygon, started collecting antiquarian books, not only approved the suggestion but found a very early Edward VI example as the proposed gift.

Frederick's life had several clearly marked periods of development. There was his upbringing by Miss Marks, who unwittingly inculcated in him his love of ritual by her exploration of the various chapels that were built in London as a direct result of the Tractarian Movement; his time at Eton, when he began to acquire his exceptional fluency in Latin and his knowledge of medieval books. He was President of the Oxford Union in 1851 and became Fellow of All Souls' College in 1852, but in 1864 because of the worsening of his brother's health he resigned and returned to Madresfield, whilst Henry went to live at Brighton in the hope of some improvement in his illness. Frederick had also to learn—very quickly—about the administration of the estates, for he had now to face the prospect of succeeding since Henry was unmarried. He had also to cope with the deaths during 1864-5 of the three women who had been closest to him as long as he could remember—his sister Georgiana, Miss Susan their old nurse and Miss Marks the stern governess who had ruled the Court since 1853 as housekeeper.

One of his first acts was to complete the building of Madresfield's third church, designed by Frederick Preedy, to replace the disaster of Pugin's attempt at a second. Then Frederick built the almshouses and church at Newland in fulfilment of the promise of their uncle, the third earl, to his first wife. Apart from his genuine philanthropy,

Frederick had a passion for architecture, and he showed a practical interest in every building project he undertook. He also undertook an associated activity which another man, if any other would indeed have conceived the idea in the first place, might well have postponed till later.

In the summer of 1866, having arranged that in March Henry should be buried close to the site of the new church, Frederick obtained faculties for the exhumation and reburial of several other members of his family. He brought his mother, Lady Susan Eliot, from Cornwall, his sister Lady Georgiana Raglan, from Wales, Miss Susan Marks from London and Miss Marks from Malvern, and also transferred the remains of his father to the new graveyard. This was done over a period of six weeks—two each Saturday morning at 6a.m., the graves being dug by older gardeners who could be relied on not to gossip, and with the rector in attendance to hallow the new graves. He had also, since Henry's death, been converting two rooms in the Court to form a small private chapel, and this work was now completed.

As soon as Frederick had fulfilled his duty, as he doubtless saw it, towards his departed relatives and others, he turned his mind at last to his own future. It is apparent from correspondence that he had at some time made a private vow of celibacy, in the hope that what was called a Uniate Church might evolve in which Canterbury would be in communion with Rome, and that if and when this happened he might be ordained a priest. But it had now become evident that this hope was unlikely to materialise within his lifetime, and in view of the changes in his own life and his inheritance, he asked for advice from Henry Parry Liddon, whom he had invited for the weekend of Advent Sunday in December, 1866, as to whether he could be released from his vow. At Oxford, Liddon had been one of his first acquaintances—a young clergyman, recently ordained, and only a year or two older than himself. So began a friendship which was to last for the rest of their lives, for Frederick died only a few months after Liddon. Whilst at Christ Church, Liddon introduced him to Dr. E.B. Pusey and his circle, and before long his potential value to the Tractarians was recognised. Liddon thought this release possible but agreed to seek a ruling from Pusey. A few days later Liddon wrote to Frederick to say that Pusey had judged that as it had been only a

Some of the almshouses at Newland

private promise of celibacy rather than a public vow, he did not require formal dispensation from it, and that because of Frederick's new situation it was in fact his duty to marry and to become instead of a priest a good Christian landowner and employer.

Frederick's response was swift. He had already had an invitation to spend Christmas with Lord Stanhope (Philip Stanhope, the historian) and his wife at their home at Chevening; now he wrote to accept. The next letter in the sequence says it all. Addressed to their only daughter, Lady Mary and dated 6 January, (the Epiphany), 1867, it began 'My dearest, I went to Holy Communion this morning at 8.30a.m. to thank God for giving you to me ...'

It was more than another year before they were married, and the marriage was to prove idyllic. She was a very intelligent woman who, idolised by her parents, had had an exceptionally wide-ranging education for her time. She was fluent in several languages. There is a well-attested story of her

The church at Newland

sitting, at six years old, on the Duke of Wellington's knee when he was entertaining some male friends with a somewhat risqué story when, noting the child's quick comprehension, he hurriedly switched to French only to be disconcerted to find that she quite understood the purport of what he was saying and laughed heartily. Another early admirer had been Macaulay, who composed for her his verse 'There was a little girl Who had a little curl Right in the middle of her forehead, And when she was good She was very, *very* good, But when she was bad she was horrid.' There certainly are many instances of her life as Lady Beauchamp which indicate that she was indeed very good, but none which suggests otherwise. She was, like so many other Victorian wives, full of good works, and she founded an Industrial School in the village, which continued until 1931, and which took in orphaned or abandoned girls between the ages of 6 and 14, training them as domestic helps, cooks and laundresses, who at the age of 14 were sent out to the great houses in various parts of England. One or two even succeeded in business on their own account—one ran her own laundry in Gloucester. Another married a young gardener on the estate; their son, Arthur T. Weston, who attributed his success to the strict sense of duty and service which his

Lady Mary Stanhope, Countess Beauchamp

mother had learned at the Madresfield Industrial School, eventually went, via scholarships, to Manchester Grammar School and university, to India, ending his career as Director of Industries for Bengal.

Lady Beauchamp was a gifted artist, which is evidenced by the many drawings and paintings she left. She also used these gifts in refurnishing and redecorating the Court, and her husband paid warm tribute to her share in the work of bringing new life to the house which had been somewhat neglected, having been without a proper chatelaine for many years. But she died in childbirth after little more than eight years of marriage, in June 1876, leaving two sons and three daughters.

It was also a time of grief due to the death of Prince Albert, when the depth of sorrow sometimes seems to have been measured by the width of the black border on the letters of condolence. Those on the numerous letters which the young Earl Beauchamp received from high and low were no exception. He carefully preserved them all, making no differentiation between the social standing of the senders, except in one instance: At the bottom of the box in which he stored them all, he put three, carefully folded within a sheet of the thickest notepaper he possessed.

The first bore the address 'Cumberland Lodge, Windsor Gt. Park' and had been written by Queen Victoria's fifth child, Helena, wife of Prince Christian of Schleswig-Holstein, whose week-old baby had died just a month previously. She began her letter, like everyone else, with a plea to be forgiven 'for intruding on you in these first hours of your terrible, bitter sorrow', but then abruptly she discarded formality and continued:

> How dearly I loved your dear Mary I think I could not tell you, nor the true friendship I bore her, and her loss is a very great grief to me. Only a few weeks ago she sent me such loving words of sympathy on the loss of my darling little Child - and now she

too is gone to that Land of everlasting peace and joy. Forgive me for having said too much, and believe how truly my tears are flowing with yours.

Then as though recollecting her rank, she ended formally 'With every renewed expression of the truest sympathy from the Prince and myself, Believe me, Yours most truly, Helena, Princess Christian etc. Princess of Great Britain and Ireland.'

The second letter was very different. Headed 'Marlborough House' and signed 'Albert Edward', it was a formal expression of condolence from the Prince of Wales on Lord Beauchamp's 'terrible and irreparable loss'. Although of a similar age, the pleasure-loving prince had little in common with the deeply-religious and rather austere earl.

The third letter was one of four pages covered in spidery writing, difficult to decipher, heavily underlined and bespattered with exclamation marks. It was of course, unsigned, since the queen usually wrote to her ministers in the third person. She wrote from Windsor Castle:

> The Queen hardly knows how to write to Lord Beauchamp on the occasion of the dreadful misfortune which has befallen him, or how to find words to express her deep and true sympathy with him in this hour of awful bereavement! All the Queen can say, is - that having _herself_ gone through the _same_ terrible trial, she is _able_ to understand his present sufferings and to feel deeply for him!
>
> His dear wife was so charming and gifted, that she was universally beloved, and the Queen will ever retain a pleasing recollection of her visit here!
>
> The severe blows she sustained in losing both her dear Parents within so short a time, were no doubt too much for her. She seemed so devoted to her dear Father whose death was so sudden. They were so proud of her!
>
> The Queen sincerely hopes that God may support and in His own good time comfort Lord Beauchamp and his dear Children.

Lord Stanhope had died shortly after Lady Stanhope in 1875; Frederick, then having no close relatives of his own, had become very much attached to them after his marriage—in fact Lord Stanhope had stayed for a long period at Madresfield Court after his wife's death.

Lady Beauchamp had expressed the hope that in the event of her death her husband would remarry in the interests of the children, and, possibly remembering his own experience at the hands of a governess when his father decided to remain a widower, Frederick married in 1878 Lady Emily Pierrepoint, daughter of the third Earl Manvers. By her he had two sons and two daughters.

The Churchman

Whilst at Eton Frederick seems to have been influenced, as he had already been by Miss Marks' leanings, by his house master, Mr. Okes. He went up to Oxford in a highly emotional state, for his sister Felicia, who had in some respects taken the place of their mother ever since she had died when he was only six years old, was buried on the day he left for university, and he was not allowed to attend her funeral. It was during this period that he met Liddon and Pusey, as mentioned, and became involved with those who were seeking to revive the Religious Life in the Church of England, which had been dormant since the Dissolution of the Monasteries three centuries earlier. As early as 1838 a straight translation of the Breviary had been proposed; a few years later a translation of a few portions was published, bound in brown paper and sold in Oxford. But for several reasons this was considered quite inadequate and it did not receive general acceptance by the Tractarians. Several other attempts were made, but still did not meet with general approval. Frederick Lygon was therefore consulted on the matter, however for political reasons he was unable at first to allow his name to be associated with the project. The necessity for an authoritative work was agreed, but when Rev. J.M. Neale—another prominent Tractarian and the founder of the Community of the Sisters of the Church at East Grinstead—tried to pressurise Frederick into supporting the revival of religious communities in 1855, he met at first with firm resistance. Frederick had been elected a Member of Parliament as a follower of Disraeli, and had been appointed as a Lord of the Admiralty in 1859. Gladstone supported such a revival, whilst Disraeli opposed it; it would have been most inappropriate to allow the name of a Lygon holding a Government appointment to be associated with the Opposition's viewpoint. In addition, so far as the Church was concerned, Neale had the reputation of being something of a hothead.

Eventually Frederick agreed to attempt the project. It was a task for which he was well qualified and he undertook it with enthusiasm, its sources lying exactly in Frederick's favourite area of study—ancient and medieval texts. To this day the library at Madresfield Court contains a fine collection of missals, vesper books and other manuscripts dating from the 13th century, which were invaluable in his work (although a

Frederick, Sixth Earl Beauchamp

representative of one of England's great auction houses recently dismissed them as 'of no value nowadays; there's no money in religion to-day.') Only a handful of influential churchmen knew of the proposal, but Frederick kept them informed of his progress, often sending his translations of prayers and ancient hymns to several scholars, both Anglican and Roman Catholic, for their comments. In particular, he was obliged to be especially careful in the translation of the prayers in order not to conflict with specific Anglican doctrines; direct invocation of saints, for example, had to be avoided. His work was published in 1858 with a number of safeguards in its title: *The Day Hours of the Church of England, newly translated and arranged according to the Prayer Book and the Authorised Version of the Bible.* Great emphasis was laid upon the fact that the compiler had based his work on the Sarum (Salisbury) Use, which it was hoped would commend it to Church of England clergymen and hopefully distance it from suspect Roman influences. The most ancient records of Christianity in England, preserved in the diocese of Salisbury, pre-date the Norman Conquest by some five centuries, and therefore showed what had been the established practice before Rome had asserted ecclesiastical control, so that the High Church party could not be accused of attempting to revive merely pre-Reformation customs. An innovation was the inclusion of several blank pages on which any community could include its own particular prayers, and lay people were also encouraged to make use of 'the book according to their own inclination'. The book was also compiled bearing in mind the revival of the Religious Life in the Church of England—i.e. not only the rebirth of monastic life lived in the community, but the needs of those who, being unable for genuine reasons to undertake the communal life, yet wished to live a life of strict and regulated devotion in their accustomed surroundings. This often included either the taking of vows or at least the making of a solemn promise, and living henceforward under direction in spiritual matters by a priest. In fact, just the sort of life—despite his sometimes high profile in Society—which Frederick himself had attempted before his succession to the title and his marriage.

The emerging Communities of monks and nuns, and some devout laypeople, were delighted to have at last an Office Book, which although the Church of England was still somewhat ambivalent on the subject, was generally conceded to have been based on sound scholarship and to contain little or nothing offensive to conscientious Anglicans. Copies were sent to each community, at first without charge (Frederick personally bore all the cost); it was only many years later that he charged one shilling (5p.) a copy.

Frederick cherished the letters of congratulation he received from the few who knew the secret of the book's authorship, especially the messages which came from prominent Roman Catholic theologians, though he never acknowledged his authorship outside his own close circle. The book was also well-received by many Anglican dignitaries; E.F. Benson, Archbishop of Canterbury, probably represented many when he wrote later that 'I have always been very thankful for the Day Hours and have used it for years in our Domestic Chapels at Lincoln and Truro. I have thought the book was doing a great deal of good and opening the door to much more good in familiarising the church people with the to them hazy fact that there was more to come from the sources from which the Prayer Book came.'

The Day Hours went into five editions, each of 5,000 copies, and shortly before his death he ordered a new edition of 7,000 copies, which was to be illustrated with woodcuts from his manuscript collection. After his death the book was taken over and amended versions published by communities at both Wantage and Cowley. Dr. Pusey had taken a great interest in the production of this book for a rather poignant reason—his own young daughter had hoped to be among the first in the Anglican Church to take the three traditional vows but she died at the age of 12, and as he related afterwards he had charged her 'to pray in heaven for the restoration of the Religious Life in the Church of England.'

Frederick was keenly interested in the organisation of various forms of religious communities, and amongst his papers is a draft of the Constitution he prepared in response to a request from the newly-formed Society of the Holy and Undivided Trinity—a women's community which no longer exists—and a very considerable amount of correspondence dealing with the foundation of Keble College, with whose Constitution he was also closely associated. With Liddon, who had been appointed biographer of Pusey, leader of the Anglo-Catholic movement in later years, he was also very much involved in the establishment of Pusey House, Oxford, as his memorial.

Frederick was a member of several commissions throughout his life on various aspects of Education, Child Welfare, Local Government, as well as specifically Church matters, such as Ritual, and The Use of the Athanasian Creed, though here he seems to have been in a minority of one in advocating its continued retention in the saying of Matins. He was an active member of the Church Assembly, forerunner of the General Synod. His keen interest in music led to enthusiasm for the restoration of Gregorian plainsong in church services, and to the founding of the Gregorian Society; he is said to have published settings for at least three anthems, though unfortunately these seem to have been lost. But his setting of what has been called 'the Lygon Psalm', because from it was taken their traditional motto 'The lot is fallen unto me in a fair ground: yea, I have a goodly heritage' (Ps. 16, v.7 in the translation used in the Book of Common Prayer) was sung after his death when his eldest son celebrated his coming of age at a service in Worcester Cathedral. As a young man Frederick also published three ballads.

Through Pusey, Frederick had been introduced to the great John Keble, an honour which the young man prized greatly, especially since like many others he regarded Keble as an English saint. Keble (1792-1866) was an Anglican theologian and poet who is credited with the initiation of the Oxford Movement, both by a sermon on 'National Apostasy' in 1833 and his subsequent publication of *Seven Tracts for the Times*, and by his scholarly works. His aim was to restore to the Church in England a sense of its continuity with its earliest roots and its spiritual heritage, which seemed to have been lost especially in the preceding three centuries. He also became famous for his poetry and his hymns; he published anonymously in 1827 a collection under the title *The Christian Year*, which was remarkably successful. But he was always careful to avoid the extremes of the Anglo-Catholic activists and their opponents. His appeal was both to ordinary people in the simplicity of his devotion, and to scholars in the wide range of his learning. In 1974 his name was added to the Church of England Calendar, where he is commemorated on 29 March as 'Priest, Pastor, Poet'. Keble visited Madresfield more than once and left, as was his custom, a handwritten poem on the back of one of his host's envelopes. From one or two phrases, it seems that Keble must have written it as he viewed the Malvern Hills from the front of the Court, close to the first old church where several of Frederick's more immediate forbears were buried. The establishment of Keble College, Oxford, founded in his memory at the suggestion of the leaders of the Oxford Movement, became the chief concern of Frederick Lygon for some years.

During the autumn of 1856 Frederick went abroad on holiday with a brother of Edward Lear, the poet and painter. Sidney Lear was considering ordination and like Frederick was deeply interested in the current religious controversies. They both did not hesitate to seek advice from Pusey, via Liddon, as to how far they might go in sharing in Roman Catholic worship whilst away from England, and were frequently advised to proceed with great caution in view of the prevailing climate at home. The suspicion attributed to Roman Catholics at the time was well illustrated by a letter to Frederick from his elder brother Henry towards the end of January 1856:

> ... I can't help being afraid that you have more than a simple design in going abroad and learning in Italian. I have still a sufficiently good opinion of you to believe that if you told me anything it would be the truth, and I assure you I should be sorry to misrepresent you in any respect, but I have a most serious distrust of you as to the <u>Protestant belief,</u> the more as perhaps you know my opinion on <u>that head</u>. I hold that no <u>really sensible man</u> can halt in the middle and that you must be a Roman Catholic or follow a Hume, Gibbon, etc. etc. Such are my notions! You always view my views so superciliously that I cannot but mistrust, because I know I am sufficiently intelligent to understand any doctrine or feeling you might have, more especially as it has been rather a study with me to view religion in all its different phases and effects. I write these lines because I do not wish any misunderstanding to exist between us. You can notice them or not as you like.
> Yr. affecte. brother Henry.

Frederick was not unduly disturbed by this letter. He wrote by return to his sister Georgiana 'I had a letter from Henry last week in which he expressed a fear that I have "more than a simple design in going abroad and learning in Italian" very kind of him but childishly absurd - don't tell him I have passed this on to you but the joke is too good to be kept.' To Henry he wrote in a more conciliatory vein: 'I can't quite understand what dark suspicions about me have been floating in your mind to induce you to give the grave caution in your last letter about my becoming a Roman - you don't really think one would be more likely to go over to the Roman by means of the Italian tongue rather than the French or English or that greater facilities are afforded in France or Italy for a traveller to take that step rather than in England ...'

Frederick was no doubt completely sincere in so writing to his anxious brother, but he perhaps did not pay sufficient regard to the family's worries after his cousin Charles Pakenham's conversion only a couple of years previously, and he certainly did not foresee what the immediate future held when, at the end of his stay in France, he went on alone to Rome to indulge his passionate interest in church architecture and art.

Left to himself, he spent his days in exploring all the ancient monuments of Rome. He also had two brief meetings with Charles Pakenham who was studying at the English College. It seems probable that it was through him he was introduced to Monsignor Howard (1829-1892), who as well as being a scion of the Duke of Norfolk's family had served as an officer in the Guards under General Edward Lygon. But his next letter to his sister reveals another development which, probably fortunately, he did not share with his brother.

At first Frederick seems to have been delighted with his new acquaintance. However, it was a short-lived delight. Mgr. Howard apparently soon decided to capture Frederick Lygon for his church, as was only to be expected since his Pakenham cousin had already capitulated, and he started a campaign for Frederick's conversion by correspondence, which was more convenient than relying on their occasional social meetings. Frederick somehow omitted to tell his family anything more than that Mgr. Howard '... was in the 2nd Life Guards and is now an ecclesiastic. He claimed to be a great friend of Henry's ...'

A few days previously, Frederick had written to his sister:

> ... We arrived here on Saturday night, the Romans have lost no time in assaulting me but I keep as clear as I can - I am much amused at the snares of the Romans but think I am too old to be caught with such chaff [he was 26]. I am much disappointed in Rome but it will not do to judge hastily. I think I had put myself into an impartial frame of mind, but nevertheless could not, at first sight, nor can I now after repeated visits, appreciate St Peter's. Of course, its size is enormous and its material costly, and the construction skill very great, but as a building, much less as a Church, the result is far from satisfactory ... Tell him [Henry] I quite recant my weakness for Italian Churches, and am still a stern and staunch Mediaevalist. S. Peter's has quite disillusioned me. I went to see Charles Pakenham on Sunday. He was very cheery ...

At first Frederick responded happily to the priest, always willing to discuss and argue any matter of mutual interest. But that was not sufficient for Mgr. Howard, who was a totally committed evangelist for his cause. His letters—there are about a dozen of them, some of them of over 12 pages closely written—show him as becoming more and more desperate as he battled for this capture, which would have been quite sensational, for Frederick's elder brother, the heir presumptive, showed no inclination for marriage, and therefore one day Frederick would be very rich, very eligible and even more the 'catch' of the London season, as indeed he already was.

Frederick's replies to Mgr. Howard grew shorter each time he replied. At last Mgr. Howard sent the longest letter of all, arguing about various fundamental doctrines of the Christian faith as interpreted by Anglicans. Frederick drafted his reply and this time sent it to Liddon asking for his and Pusey's confirmation that his arguments were all valid. Liddon confirmed by return of post that both he and Pusey could find no fault with the draft.

Frederick sent his letter to Mgr. Howard, but coincidentally he received that day a letter from his sister Georgy warning him that the chief subject of gossip in their London circle was that 'Frederick Lygon is about to convert' (to Roman Catholicism) and he had better write at once and put his father's mind at rest for the General was very alarmed. She added that the General was about to offer the living of Madresfield to a clergyman not at all of Frederick's way of thinking, and he must act quickly to avoid disaster. This letter was accompanied by one from his brother declaring his undying devotion to the Anglican way and with dire comments on what he supposed to be Freddy's easily influenced mind.

By the next day's post Frederick had a 12-page epistle from Mgr. Howard. It is an extraordinary document, written in great distress at Frederick's announcement that he definitely had no intention of leaving the Anglican church. There is much evidence of Mgr. Howard's genuine concern for Frederick's spiritual welfare, but this is rather eclipsed by the somewhat naive threats of eternal hellfire and torment.

Frederick replied very briefly, to say he had been called home on urgent business. He arrived in time to persuade his father to offer the Madresfield living to the Rev. G.S. Munn, a friend of the Lear family and a sympathiser with the Tractarians, and as he stayed for nearly 50 years, Frederick never had to face a similar crisis in later years.

There is no indication that he and Mgr. Howard ever met again, but some years later the priest, (made a cardinal in 1881), sent him a holy picture accompanied by polite condolences on the death of his wife. And later Frederick indirectly returned the compliment—the Benedictine nuns at nearby Stanbrook Abbey were having Cardinal Manning (an erstwhile Anglican Archdeacon) to consecrate their building, so Frederick, now Lord Beauchamp, not only invited him to stay at the Court, but put at his disposal his best carriage and pair, plus coachman and two grooms, all adorned with red rosettes in honour of the guest's rank. But Malvern, that nice genteel town, was deeply offended, and its citizens wrote to their local paper demanding an explanation of the earl's actions, so unsuitable for a leading Anglican.

What might almost be described as another 'hobby' of Frederick, was his addiction to building new churches, often at his sole expense. He built them in Worcestershire, Gloucestershire, and Lincolnshire, in Wimbledon, Pimlico and Hackney, and also restored a number of others which had distant Beauchamp connections. New churches were always accompanied by village schools wherever possible, for he had a passionate enthusiasm for education for the young. In addition, he was deeply involved with the founding of the Boys' College in Malvern and the Alice Ottley School for Girls in Worcester.

The Politician

Both Frederick and his elder brother Henry had been well-known to Disraeli from their childhood and he professed a great regard for them. It was Frederick, however, who had a practical interest in politics and who became M.P. for Tewkesbury in 1857, and, after his brother succeeded to the title, M.P. for Worcestershire from 1863 to 1866.

There is a vivid and not altogether friendly glimpse of him as a member of the House in *The Times* in 1869, some 12 years after he first became an M.P. and three years after taking his seat in the Lords. A retrospective look at the last decade, it chose to illustrate Beauchamp's debut in Parliament by recalling an incident when the newcomer had, perhaps rather unwisely, chosen to accuse a senior opponent of what would now be described as sleaze:

> In 1857 [Mr Lygon] was elected, in 1859 he became a Lord of the Admiralty! It was a rapid rise. Why Mr Lygon so soon obtained the important post we cannot say. Perhaps he had special abilities for such an office, or perhaps it was because he was the son of Earl Beauchamp. Authorities differ. Mr Lygon's term of office was, though, a very short one. He entered in March, and left, when the Derby Government was ousted, in June. But, short as it was, it was not only [*sic*] long enough to give him a taste of the dignity, and honour, and efficiency, of the department which he had managed. Perhaps, indeed, he has felt more of this interest since he left office than he did when he held it. Indeed, the deep interest which placemen out of place feel in the efficiency of the public departments, as compared to that which they appear to feel when they are in office, is something remarkable. However, we have no fault to find with Mr Lygon's performance of his duties, for we know nothing about it. Be this as it may, he has certainly felt a deep interest in the Admiralty ever since he ceased to be 'a Lord'; for on the ground of that three months' term of office he has generally sat on the front Opposition bench, amongst the chiefs. Whenever Admiralty matters have been before the House he has always appeared with a bundle of papers in his hand; has been very active - not to say fidgety - and forward in putting questions and offering criticisms; and, last week, went so far as formally to impeach the present Secretary of the Admiralty, Lord Clarence Paget ...

As it transpired, Lord Clarence Paget was able immediately to clear himself of the charge, and *The Times* admits the genuineness of Frederick's joining in the cheering which followed his reply, but it still concluded that '... Mr Lygon ... is a very smart man in his way. His dress is perfect, and his neckties are the admiration of the House. His appearance one night as he stood at the bar was, from the Reporters' Gallery, quite dazzling, for he sported a capacious scarf of brilliant scarlet, which covered his breast, and, contrasting as it did with his white waistcoat, and flashing in the gaslight, made him look quite meteoric.'

When Gladstone himself was defeated by a Conservative candidate, Gathorne Hardy, at Oxford in the General Election of 1865, Disraeli congratulated Frederick on 'an historical event which I believe to be mainly, if not entirely, owing to your resolution and energy.' It did indeed owe much to Frederick's enthusiasm, for he played a large part in organising support for Gathorne Hardy.

A few years later Frederick suggested to Disraeli that it might be useful to publish a collection of his speeches on matters concerning the Church of England, and volunteered to edit it. Disraeli accepted the offer with enthusiasm, and replied; 'No one but you could be the editor, as you know my inmost mind, and there is entire sympathy between us.' The time needed a High Churchman like Frederick for the task, for the union of Church and State was threatened as it had not been for centuries; as Frederick wrote in his (anonymous) preface: 'Measures were astutely devised either to sap some ancient buttress which supported, or to pull down some stately pinnacle which adorned, the venerable fabric of the Established Church. Distinguished persons in high places, aghast at these new dangers, counselled surrender; others advocated a temporising policy; but Mr Disraeli, with rare sagacity, surveyed the position and comprehended the full consequences of yielding at such a crisis.' About this time one of the leading newspapers printed an article congratulating the country on possessing in Disraeli a statesman who, although born a Jew, showed such an exceptional grasp of matters affecting the Anglican Church. Frederick carefully preserved this article, without comment, in one of his scrapbooks, perhaps with some wry amusement, for he wrote most of Disraeli's pronouncements on the subject.

When Disraeli returned to power in 1874, he informed the queen that he wished to appoint Lord Beauchamp, as Frederick now was, Lord Steward of the Royal Household. At first this suggestion did not meet with

Frederick, Sixth Earl Beauchamp

approval. Queen Victoria, who insisted on being regarded as holding Broad Church views, did not wish to have any holder of Anglo-Catholic persuasion in daily contact with herself or her family. The same objection was also applicable to the Marquess of Bath, whom Disraeli wanted as Lord Chamberlain. Eventually the queen reluctantly agreed, with the proviso that whilst holding office neither would take any prominent part in Church politics. She added that:

> It is considered desirable that this condition should be clearly understood, as she looks upon the views of the Church party with which Lord Beauchamp is connected, as detrimental to the interests of the Church of England, and dangerous to the Protestant religion. The Queen therefore could give no countenance to that party by admitting a prominent member of it into the Royal Household.

Disraeli discussed the matter with Lord Salisbury, writing that:

> I shall say nothing to Beauchamp himself, lest he throw up his appointment in an ecclesiastical pet which would be only cutting his own throat, and whatever may be his faults of manner and temper, he is a thorough good fellow, as I believe we both feel. But I wish you would consider all this and give me your advice. You might perhaps say things as a friend to him which might be harder to bear from an official chief. I think with tact, and thorough understanding between you and others, the ship may be steered thro' all these Church and religious sandbanks and shallows, but I see that vigilance is requisite. Greater trials will arise than the appointment of a Lord Steward or a Lord Chamberlain.

Salisbury replied:

> I will speak if you think it desirable to both Beauchamp and Bath on this point. I am sure they will feel it a matter of duty not to be themselves ... [involved] in church matters in a sense disapproved of by the Queen, so long as they are closely connected with her immediate service. The argument - if I may venture to suggest it - which will weigh with her most strongly, I believe, against too decided measures is that this Ritualist party, though not preponderant in numbers, is numerous enough, if it goes against the Establishment, to turn the scale. It is earnest, to fanaticism: it sits loosely to the Establishment, as matters stand; and if driven by any act of serious aggression, will listen to its most serious advisors and throw itself on the Free Church side. A disruption in England will not perhaps take place for so light a matter as that which took place in Scotland, but if it should take place, it will bring the whole fabric of the Church down about our ears.

It is difficult for us at the end of the 20th century to appreciate how vitally important religious practice was in every sphere of life in Victorian times. It seems as though belief was not quite so important as how that belief was put into practice; flowers and incense, and candles beyond the strictly essential, were anathema to the queen in church, and Beauchamp, with his love of ritual and ceremonial in church, entered on his public career in politics considerably handicapped. Perhaps his saving grace, from the Royal viewpoint, was that he had married a Lady in Waiting who was very much in favour and was also a close friend of the queen's fifth daughter Helena Louise.

Beauchamp was kept busy as Lord Steward. The Royal Household was no sleepy backwater but it was sometimes a hothouse of gossip and dissent, and although the duties of the Lord Steward were very largely concerned with the administration of the Household, the position was no sinecure. In addition, there were a number of visits from lesser foreign royalty as marriage prospects for the queen's numerous children were considered, and responsibility for ensuring they enjoyed their visits fell to a very great extent on his shoulders. The appointment did, however, bring him into close contact with the queen, and she seems to have appreciated his service over the six year period of his Stewardship. It ended in 1880, and his final political appointment was as Paymaster-General between 1885 and 87.

The Landowner

Frederick had little involvement with the estates until the last few years of his brother's life. But by then, Henry's health was failing and gradually Frederick was of necessity drawn into the management of their property, especially when Henry finally went to stay at Brighton in 1864.

Frederick was reluctant to leave his beloved Oxford, and there was little to encourage him in his new occupation, for Henry was a somewhat demanding overseer; he had succeeded to the title only the year before his illness developed, when there were still a number of legal matters to be decided following their father's death, and Frederick had to learn to deal with the routine as well as clearing the backlog which had accumulated. The most striking feature of their correspondence at this time is perhaps the patience with which Frederick responded to his brother's frequently unfounded complaints; it shows in a completely different light the character which the archbishop of Canterbury was later to criticise as 'chimerical'.

The earl also undertook the complete reorganisation of the Court's gardens and grounds. With regard to the gardens, he was particularly fortunate to secure the services of William Crump, who had been employed at Blenheim Palace and whose expertise resulted in Madresfield becoming well-known for a number of features: its avenues of poplars and elms; its Rock Garden—constructed largely of artificial 'rocks'; its rose garden; the development of the moat; the addition of a small waterfall and various other improvements which added to the attractiveness of the grounds. Crump became well-known in horticultural circles and an acknowledged expert especially in two fields—the cultivation of grapes and apples, the 'Madresfield Grape' and 'Crump's Apple' having been bred by him. Whilst the magnificent vine he planted at Madresfeld still flourishes, examples of the apple are harder to discover. He was responsible for the initiation of several schemes for tree and fruit culture throughout the estate and widely respected for the spread of training and knowledge about all matters horticultural throughout Worcestershire. He was awarded one of only seven Victoria Medals of Honour given for skill in horticulture to celebrate the queen's jubilee in 1897, and continued to work at Madresfield until he retired in 1919 at the age of 76.

William Crump

Frederick undertook a major reorganisation of the landholdings, selling a few small properties but purchasing several large farms and also developing some areas within Malvern itself; at one time the Estate Office was situated at the top of Malvern Link, facing Malvern Common. He also bought properties in Powick,

Newland and Callow End as well as elsewhere in south Worcestershire, but at the same time he sold a number of outlying properties with the objective of making the estate more compact.

But his main reorganisation concerned the village itself. His father had by means of a private Act of Parliament moved the main road away from the Court to its present route, and now Frederick built cottages on either side of it, with a post office and a school to complete the transformation of a scattered hamlet to an orderly Victorian village, dominated by Preedy's new church. Tucked away out of sight down a narrow lane was the early Victorian rectory, originally a fairly simple Georgian house twice enlarged to accommodate the rector's ever-increasing family, for like his patron he too was twice married and had nine children.

Frederick took a very active interest in local government, and sat on various local Boards. He was a governor of several local schools, not only church sponsored but including Malvern Boys' College and Alice

The new north lodge

Ottley Girls' School in Worcester, both of which he helped to found. He held, of course, a number of official posts. Sometimes, looking at the list, one wonders how he managed to keep in touch with them all, for he was extremely conscientious, but somehow he coped with both national and local commitments. He tried to keep Sundays free for important house guests, but he was warned that he was undertaking too much. Unfortunately he did not heed the warnings.

At Christmas 1890, there had been the usual houseful of relations and friends. They departed after New Year and he sought to catch up on his local affairs. The 18th birthday of his eldest son William fell on Saturday, 20 February, but he was due back at college the previous day. So on the 18th Frederick gave a small dinner party to celebrate. On the 19th they parted, William for Oxford and his father to attend a local government meeting at Upton-on-Severn. He returned late for lunch. It was his habit, when there were no guests, to share the children's lunch, and he was in the act of carving the joint—on these family occasions he insisted on doing this himself—when he collapsed and died instantly.

The shock was national as well as local; for so long he had been prominent in Church and State, admired or hated for his strong opinions but never ignored. Every newspaper commented; tributes flowed in; everyone expected a great gathering for his funeral. Then came another surprise. Frederick Lygon, sixth Earl Beauchamp, had laid down as the first proviso in his will that his funeral was to be private, and his grave to be unmarked; no memorial of any kind was to be erected to him.

The conditions were observed to the letter, though there were some attempts to get round the prohibition of any memorial. His was a simple funeral, attended only by family and very close friends. He was buried in an unmarked grave in Madresfield Churchyard beside his first wife—eventually his second was laid to rest at his other side—and no memorial was ever erected to him; but Malvern subsequently acquired a Frederick Road, and a Lygon Bank, and a Beauchamp Road, and Worcester Cathedral a Beauchamp Chapel though the authorities changed that in time. But on the site of Madresfield's tiny 12th century church, where its altar had stood, a tall Celtic cross was erected, bearing only his date of death. One feels that if he had had a monument, it would have had inscribed on it six words which he constantly scribbled on his papers during meetings of any kind, rather than mindless 'doodling'. They were the words of an old Lygon family motto: *Christ est mort pour nos péchés.*

E.W. Benson, the Archbishop of Canterbury who had disapproved of his churchmanship, nonetheless paid tribute to him as 'a bright gay man, very particular about his dress and brusque in his manner, and chimerical, but withal a faithful son of the Church', and a later bishop of London (Winnington-Ingram) considered that he 'should have been a bishop'. Perhaps they were both wrong; it takes a good man to be sincerely humble.

As well as the son who succeeded him, Frederick left three sons and five daughters. The younger son by his first wife, Edward Hugh, was killed (unmarried) in the Boer War in South Africa; Robert, his first son by his second wife, died in 1952, and Henry, his second son by this marriage, died unmarried in 1932.

Lady Mary Lygon (1869-1927)

Mary Lygon, Frederick's eldest child, displayed her gift of leadership very early. She was only five when an old family friend, visiting Madresfield and observing how she dealt with her younger brother, commented that whilst he hoped she would not be put out by being no longer the most important young person at the Court, he did not doubt her ability to deal competently with him and he hoped that she would 'keep him under the slipper' for many years to come.

It was a shrewd observation. As the occupants of the nursery multiplied, and later when there was a stepmother and stepbrothers and sisters, Lady Mary continued to deal competently with them all. It was not only by force of character, but she developed an unusual talent for dealing tactfully with people of all grades, and for pouring oil on difficult situations. She had inherited her father's gift for music, and by the time she was in her teens had organised both a boys' choir at the village church and another which included girls from the Industrial School her mother had founded in the village. At 15 she was in the habit of standing in when either of the teachers at the village school was absent. She also wrote and helped to produce the Christmas Play which the young Lygons put on each year—a considerable effort, for it usually included a good proportion of musical items. At first the school was commandeered for this, but rehearsals caused so much dislocation to classes that part of the stables was converted into a hall complete with stage. It became known as The Play Room, and the attendance eventually included many local people as well as house guests.

In due course Lady Mary became a Woman of the Bedchamber to the Duchess of Teck, mainly in order to provide companionship for the young Princess May, and when the latter married the then Duke of York, eventually George V, Lady Mary became her Lady-in-Waiting. Under one or another designation, this connection was to last until her death. The Duke of Teck was decidedly eccentric, and there were occasions when Lady Mary's tact was as invaluable as it had been in her own home.

But Lady Mary was above all a Worcestershire woman, proud of her Lygon ancestry and devoted to her Madresfield home. She travelled extensively, yet she was always longing to go back, even for just a day or so. Her success with the young choirs in the village had resulted in a passion for introducing music-making of every kind to rural areas. 'I am almost a semi-lunatic on the subject' she wrote, but there was nothing unbalanced about her assessment of the value of music in the villages, and the time was just right for such an initiative, thanks to the interest in folk music and dancing aroused by Miss Wakefield and Cecil Sharpe. Cecil Sharpe (1858-1924) was a definitive figure in the revival of interest in folk music of every kind, not only in England but also Australia, where he lived from 1882-92, and later in America. Possibly Lady Mary's stay in Sydney (see below) had brought his name to her attention, so that when she returned to London she was able to contact him for advice. Miss Wakefield had already spent a decade attempting to do, with considerable success, in Westmoreland what Lady Mary envisaged for Worcestershire, and was also a friend of Sharpe.

To read her letters in those early days is to trace the gradual development of her own interests. As her father's second family grew up in her footsteps, the innovation of

Lady Mary Lygon in 1905

plays performed at Christmas by the combined nine children became also concerts and mini-operas, which spilled over into other seasons when she conceived the idea, after her father's death, of forming a choir to sing at the weekly service in the tiny private chapel at the Court. This choir consisted of all the family plus as many of the servants she could persuade; too many for the gallery, the choir had to be split between gallery and pews below. This inspired another innovation: the great Dining Hall has a Minstrels' Gallery, and she decided that her choir should entertain guests, principally during dessert—presumably because by then the butler and footmen had discharged most of their proper duties and were free to give voice. By degrees the invited audience increased to such an extent that the public came by invitation (minus the dinners), and at Christmas 1893, the 'Madresfield Court Choir' entertained guests and tenants. More than 10 choirs from villages on the estate—all started by Lady Mary—totalling 230 voices, took part, with 29 instrumentalists in the orchestra. She conducted throughout, except when a chorus of 30 sang two pieces conducted by their composer, Edward Elgar. This was followed by a cantata composed by Lady Mary and her cousin the Hon. Richard Somerset. From this concert evolved the annual Madresfield Music Competitions, at first confined to local choirs but later to become a county event, and eventually (though many years later) the Malvern Festival.

Such competitions had been developed in Westmoreland during the previous decade by Mary Wakefield and it was under her guidance that Lady Mary introduced the concept to Worcestershire. The aim was 'to raise musical standards, promote glee singing, improve church choirs in small parishes and encourage sight-reading'. Frequently Lady Mary organised these competitions from London or wherever her duties to the Royals took her, once even from a state visit to Denmark. But usually she contrived to return home shortly before the event, to spend days driving, or riding her chestnut mare around the villages, encouraging and advising. She could rehearse five or six school choirs in a morning, but adults were more difficult; once she spent well over an hour 'going over the first chorus only'.

During her spells of duty at Court, she counted herself fortunate to secure four hours a day for her own interests. She played the organ at St. George's Chapel, Windsor, the piano after dinner for royal guests at Richmond, and the double bass whenever she could. She sang chorales with the Bach choir and glees with the Magpies in London, and she studied harmony and counterpoint with the rector of Sandringham. Most days she also wrote up to 80 letters, divided equally between the duchess' mail and her own private correspondence.

With all these activities, it is surprising how she maintained such close links with Worcestershire, and promoted support for amateur music-making to such an extent. But Mr. Elgar, the piano-tuner who cared for the Court's pianos, also had a shop in Worcester, and it must have benefited greatly from an increase in sales of sheet music thanks to Lady Mary's activities. Her father had started an agricultural show for his tenants in 1894, and an added attraction was the playing of the Civil-Military Band conducted by Mr. Elgar's son Frank. Another son, Edward, who played the organ at St. George's Roman Catholic church in Worcester, was a promising composer, anxious to make his name and grateful for any help forthcoming from someone who moved in royal circles.

Edward Elgar was only on the periphery of Lady Mary's circle. She was aware that as a boy he had sometimes accompanied his father on his piano-tuning visits, during which the young lad was despatched usually to play with the family of the Head Gardener. Now she was willing to help him where possible, but he was never a close friend. She did, however, always endeavour to attend the first performance of any of his major works. Biographers have speculated whether she knew of his intention to dedicate the 13th of his Enigma Variations to her. Her own account of the matter is succinct and offers an insight to their relationship. She wrote on 22 February 1899: 'I rode yesterday with Eddie [her brother] to Suckley and then went to see the Elgars, who were most pleasant. He has written some big orchestral theme and variations - and each of the latter portrays a friend. I am one called "Incognita", but I only heard this today, as he was too shy to tell me, and would not play them.' About the same time Elgar wrote to a friend: 'She is a most angelic person and I should like to please her'. Perhaps he hesitated to risk displeasing her by listing her name with those of people she scarcely knew; later he refers to her being 'as of old and always very "nice" and dear and rather severe'. At this time Elgar had just been knighted, and having difficulty in finding anyone to present his wife at Court, had approached Lady Mary who had willingly agreed.

In 1899 her brother was appointed Governor of New South Wales, and as he was still unmarried he asked for her to accompany him as his hostess. As it transpired she stayed only a few months, but it was whilst she was there that she met Cecil Sharpe, who further influenced her in her encouragement of folk dance and music.

Like her father, Lady Mary was deeply religious and took a keen interest in the Church of England. But she was also committed to what could be described as at least the beginnings of feminism. She supported women's suffrage, but she was also concerned about the restricted opportunities for women to serve in the Church of England. As early as 1904 she was a Vice President for the Society for the Propagation of the Gospel, and was elected a member of the first Missionary Council of the Church Assembly, probably in tribute to her and her brother's concern for the aborigines of Australia. However, her first

The Hon. Eddie Lygon, killed in the Boer War

The Boer War Memorial on the west wall of Madresfield Church, with the font in front

speech to the Church Assembly was based on her girlhood life in Madresfield, when she supported a proposal that the Board of Finance should sanction a grant to set up a training home for 'Moral Welfare Workers', saying that 'This most difficult branch of Church Work requires more careful preparation than any other if competent workers are to be secured', a remark that is probably rooted in her family's experience with the Industrial School, when on occasion the difficulty of finding suitable members of staff was acute.

From 1918 to the time of her death she was a member of the Central Committee for Women's Church Work. For a long time she met with little success, due mainly to the lack of interest and of finance on the part of the Church authorities, and little progress was made in the sphere of welfare work. But 'Women's Church Work' was a convenient umbrella term, and Lady Mary eventually managed to gain some response when she submitted a paper on 'Music in Villages', illustrated by the playing of folk dances and songs. Assisted by a choir, the whole committee joined in singing chants and descants. Not, of course, glees and ballads, but she had made a little progress. The mind boggles at the thought of reverend gentlemen and earnest ladies in large hats singing informally at all. Sadly the minutes of this meeting do not record whether the archbishop of Canterbury, who was in the chair, joined in the singing.

Another speech by Lady Mary to the whole Church Assembly was concerned with a different aspect of church music. New powers for parochial church councils were being proposed, but she successfully opposed that which would have given them responsibility for appointing church organists, and instead left the matter in the hands of the incumbent. A prominent legal authority, Lord Phillimore, had objected on legal grounds; her own objection, she said, was on musical grounds. As Secretary of the Church Musical Society 'which represents several hundreds of Church musicians all over the country', she reminded the Assembly that the organist was often a person of considerable education and usually small salary. Like her brother the seventh earl, Lady Mary could always be relied upon to take the part of the vulnerable, and if the appointment of the church organist had been surrendered into the hands of some village P.C.C.s, it is possible that much initiative and experimentation would have been stifled. She was Secretary of the Church Music Society from 1906, and President of the English Folk Dance Society from 1912, as well as being a member of the Church Assembly and Missionary Council.

A few years later she again spoke from her experiences in Australia, when she referred to her connection for many years with the Church Emigration Society, urging the sending out of committed Church people who would do much to strengthen Church life in the dominions.

One of the least-known of her achievements was the preparation of the Beauchamp volume for The Roxburghe Club after her brother's succession. This Club, which then consisted entirely of hereditary peers, has a requirement that each shall submit for publication some scholarly work. It was she who produced on behalf of her brother the seventh earl a study of the music of Henry VIII, which the Club published in 1910.

In 1905 she married The Hon. Walter Hepburn-Stuart-Forbes-Trefusis (which she shortened immediately to Trefusis) son of the 20th Baron Clinton, and at once proceeded to organise a County Music Festival from her new home in Cornwall. The Cornish Music Festival still survives and indeed increasingly flourishes. She died in 1927 leaving one son and three daughters. For 38 years she had served the Royal Family in an intimate capacity, and Queen Mary's Lady-in-Waiting sent a letter to her brother expressing sympathy:

> The Queen commands me to try and tell you how deeply she sympathizes with you over the loss of our beloved Mary, and how much Her Majesty feels her going. She valued Mary as her best friend as well as her faithful, devoted, clever and wonderful servant, and she is very, very sad ...

CHAPTER ELEVEN
William, Seventh Earl Beauchamp (1872-1938)

William, born on 20 February 1872, was the second child of Frederick, the sixth earl, and Lady Mary Stanhope. It is understandable that it was an occasion for much rejoicing beyond the family home. For a long time previously the future of the family at the Court had seemed so uncertain; the third earl had had no children, the fourth had only two sons of whom the elder had never married and had been in failing health for some years; and finally Frederick had so long postponed the thought of marriage and then his first child had been a girl. For a society which valued so highly the importance of inheritance and of a male heir, the birth resulted in unprecedented celebrations. It hardly needed the added incentive of the popularity of his father with the many local parishes he had befriended with new or restored churches and schools and his encouragement of universal education to ensure that, not only in the three counties of Worcestershire, Gloucestershire and Herefordshire, village churches across England who had Lord Beauchamp as their patron, rang their bells when the news was announced.

William's mother died when he was only three years old, and his father's remarriage in 1878 in due course brought more youngsters to the nursery. From the beginning, however, there was no doubt as to his unique importance; when he was only five years old his father took him to the House of Lords and sat him on the steps of the throne, as was a peer's privilege with his heir. But his elder sister Mary had the strongest influence on the growing boy. Her strong sense of duty and of service to others, and her perhaps unconscious assumption of leadership amongst the younger family, had a profound and lasting influence on him during these formative years, an influence probably stronger than even his Eton schooling. From Eton he went on to his father's old college, Christ Church, Oxford, and entered on an academic career which was to come to an abrupt end.

He was clever and articulate, and became President of the Union in due course. Then as his 19th birthday came close, in late February 1891, there was a small dinner party at Madresfield and the next day he returned to Oxford, to be summoned on arrival at college to the dean's presence. The dean, not long appointed to the office, informed him that his father had been taken 'seriously ill' and he was to return to Worcester at once.

He went to his rooms to collect his still unpacked luggage, meeting *en route* his tutor whom he later noted had seemed rather strained but had only enquired as to how the vacation had been. It was not until a couple of hours later, when he stepped off the train at Worcester, that he saw a newspaper billboard with the announcement in large letters: 'Death of Lord Beauchamp'. He bought a copy and read the story of the death. Later he cut out the article and carefully pasted it into a scrapbook, noting beside it in his clear handwriting 'This was the first intimation I had of my father's death'. It was then that he realised that the dean had only mentioned illness and his tutor had not referred at all to the matter, although they were aware that the earl was already dead. He felt it extremely difficult to forgive especially the dean for this deception, as he saw it. His tutor later explained that when he had met him in the quad, he had thought the young man was aware of the death and because he was obviously hurrying for his train had refrained from any expressions of sympathy, an explanation which William eventually accepted. But his relationship with the dean seemed irrevocably damaged.

After the funeral, he returned to Oxford to try to resume his studies. He was already following in his father's footsteps as an ardent Anglo-Catholic, but he had a strongly evangelistic streak which led him to become the Secretary of the Oxford Mission. This organisation made a point of bringing to Oxford young men from the poorer classes in London in an attempt to give them a glimpse of a very different lifestyle and so encourage them to raise their sights to a better existence than the narrow streets of the city. There is a strong tradition, though this has been impossible to verify, that on occasion the young Earl Beauchamp was seen preaching at open-air meetings in the East End under the auspices of the Salvation Army. What has been established is that he was friendly with a Salvation Army officer named Hugh Sladen, whose mother had been born Lady Sarah Lambart, grand-daughter of the eighth Earl of Cavan, a friend of the family through his service with the British Army. She had become a Salvationist after her marriage. Beauchamp remained friendly with the Sladen family for many years, and in 1913, after he was appointed Warden of the Cinque Ports, they visited him at Walmer Castle. One of the Court's scrapbooks contains an article and photograph of Mrs. Sladen, culled from a magazine *All The World*.

In 1894 came the incident, frequently misreported, which brought an abrupt end to his academic career. Beauchamp had been invited to the 21st birthday party of a member of the Duke of Marlborough's family; almost certainly the coming of age celebrations for the heir to the dukedom. The dean of Christ Church had refused Beauchamp and a friend permission to attend, but, as two hot-headed young men, they decided to defy his refusal and joined the celebrations at Blenheim Palace. Subsequently they were confronted by an extremely angry dean, who sent the friend down for the remainder of the term, but as Beauchamp refused to apologise he was expelled.

Since the incident of his father's death and the brief chat with the dean when he withheld the fact that the sixth earl was already dead, Beauchamp had developed a deep distrust of the dean. Now he returned to Madresfield in considerable distress; his health suffered badly and he was advised to go on a cruise to recuperate. He spent several months cruising in the Mediterranean, with a stay in Madeira. It was fortunate, however, that his father had named his brother-in-law, Edward Stanhope, as his own executor and his heir's trustee until he should come of age. Edward Stanhope and other members of the Stanhope family with their wide humanitarian interests seem to have had a strong influence on the young Earl. His coming-of-age was the cause of great celebrations at Madresfield, even though these were considerably overshadowed by memories of his father's death. Now he was able to take his seat in the House of Lords and sat nominally as a Unionist (the Conservative and Unionist parties had united some years previously), perhaps out of respect for his father, that staunch supporter of Disraeli. For the first and only time in his life, in September, 1893, he voted against Home Rule for Ireland, which the Unionists were desperate to crush. Twenty years later he was to refer to this incident with some bitterness when speaking in support of Asquith's Bill for Home Rule, recalling having been 'dragged from somewhat fruitless studies at Oxford' to vote against Gladstone's Bill on the same matter.

Having left Oxford without completing his studies proved to be no handicap in his entry into public affairs. In 1895 he was elected as Mayor of Worcester, the first peer ever to be so chosen in England, and this was followed by election to Worcestershire County Council in the same year. Minutes of both bodies indicate that he took his duties very seriously indeed and ruffled not a few feathers in so doing. He also became a member of the London Board of Education, so signalling his impending movement into the national arena. At the time *The Christian Review* described him as 'tinged with Christian Socialism'. But Beauchamp was already widely popular, recognised as a man of wide sympathies who could mix with all classes and yet retain his dignity. Many years later, in 1936, there is a true story of how the earl would often take himself to his Head Gardener's house where he would share morning coffee or afternoon tea with his employee and his wife to escape, as he put it, 'the emptiness of that big house'.

Perhaps an early indication of where his sympathies would lie throughout his life was shown by the garden party he gave in the grounds of the Court in April, 1898, for the National Union of Teachers, formed in 1870. There was a long programme of music, the first part of which was played at The Rocks, a feature built in the grounds by his father, and the second in front of the house, the Civil-Military Band of Worcester being conducted

Earl Beauchamp wearing Worcester's mayoral chain

by Frank Elgar, brother of the composer. The occasion seems to have included a tour of the Court, for with the programme are four pages of notes both about the Gardens and also describing various interior features of the house.

By the autumn of 1898 he was already frequently chafing at not having been given 'a man's job to do', as he expressed it, though it was later suggested that his radical opinions somewhat alarmed the Conservative government led by Joseph Chamberlain. For this reason the *Leeds Mercury* supposed that Beauchamp's appointment at the tender (politically speaking) age of 27 as Governor and Commander-in-Chief of New South Wales might be Chamberlain's ruse to remove such a potentially dangerous member of the Upper House from London for a while, whilst the *Daily Mail* saw it as one of a series of appointments at the same time as 'experimental, interesting and original'.

The appointment was a surprise to him, but not to two of his sisters. Lady Mary, now a lady-in-waiting to Princess May, wife of the Duke of York, and Lady Margaret, wife of the second Lord Ampthill who held a post in the Colonial Office, were informed in the late autumn of 1899 of the intended proposal to send their brother abroad, but both were too well-trained to have dreamt of giving him the slightest hint in advance of the official announcement. When at last it came, on New Year's Day, 1899, they both wrote to congratulate him and the spontaneity of their letters is outstanding amongst the many letters of congratulation and good wishes he received. He himself could hardly credit the news. And inevitably, just as Macaulay had been credited with writing a rhyme about his mother, so now Hilaire Belloc is said to have had her son in mind in his *Cautionary Tales*, when he commented on Lord Lundy with the words 'My language fails! Go out and govern New South Wales!' But the ridicule was unjustified. Eventually Beauchamp would display a far stronger character than anyone seems as yet to have suspected.

He was to sail in April, and this resulted in a fine flurry of preparation. Sometimes ambassadors and governors helped to furnish their residences, and Madresfield Court was temporarily stripped of some of its French and Italian treasures; many of the fine pictures were packed, as well as most of the family silver and other items of daily use. This was not, he emphasised later, in any attempt to impress the colonials but rather to a genuine desire to share with others some of the possessions that gave him so much delight. He needed an aide-de-camp, and was keen to take with him his brother Eddie, but he unfortunately had already volunteered for service in South Africa—a year later he was one of the Boer War's fatalities. He also asked for permission to take with him as his hostess his sister Lady Mary, and this was reluctantly conceded; she was still extremely useful to the Tecks. Possibly the unkindest comment came from the ageing Queen Victoria when she heard of this request. She is alleged to have remarked: 'Well, I suppose he must take his nanny with him'.

Lady Mary was overjoyed. Her work with the Royals was no sinecure. She was expected to serve at least nine months in each year—nine months of 24 hours every day on duty—and even the three months' leave of absence could be, and was quite frequently, over-ruled. To go abroad with her favourite brother, and to such an unknown country as Australia then was, seemed to her an enormous favour.

There is a little-known account of the arrival of the novice statesman at the quayside in Sydney. Faced with a quayside reception and dressed up in all the unaccustomed glory of a uniform complete with tricorn hat and plumes, he desperately sought to hide behind a tall photographer for fear he would make a mistake as he acknowledged for the first time the official salute of a guard of honour. Remembering how utterly inexperienced he was in such grand occasions, the wonder is that he so quickly became accustomed to them.

There followed a fairly hectic five months mainly of receptions and banquets for them both, coupled with some political work for Beauchamp and his first venture into the outback—probably an older and wiser public servant would have avoided involvement in domestic politics, but that was not his nature, and soon his radical opinions had made him both friends and enemies.

As always, he was outspoken in his advocacy of Christianity in practice as well as in profession. In a speech in August, 1899, he condemned the dangers of identifying Christianity with Imperialism, and, even now when Imperialism has vanished and Christianity greatly declined, bearing in mind recent attempts by the indigenous population to claim their rights Beauchamp's words illustrate his foresight:

The earl in Australian uniform

> It is not fair ... to treat natives who have only just been made Christians by the ideal standard of Christian experience. If only these critics would test our native Christians by the standard of their own Christianity there would not be much to fear ... After all, for us, who have had many years of Christianity, we have nothing to boast about and nothing to be proud of, and we ... may learn a lesson from the natives of the Islands ... Our present policy is that we should dot the world over with knots of Imperial officers in the centres of population ... A policy like that must lead to a policy of force and repression and war unless we also send out those who will preach not only the gospel of trade, but the Gospel of love and Christianity.

Within two months, exhausted by the initial whirlwind pressure of the Governor's duties, he undertook his first journey under the somewhat mistaken impression that it would offer some respite from the official round in Sydney. This was a visit in July to Narabri, Moree and Midkin close to the north-western boundary of his territory with Queensland; shortly afterwards he crossed the Great Dividing

Range to Forbes. He travelled mostly by a special train, which had a powerful searchlight fitted to scare away any animals on the line, for of course there were vast acreages of unfenced land. At virtually every small settlement he took care to stop and meet the locals; larger settlements insisted on giving him what they could in the shape of an official reception, and in every case he met with enormous enthusiasm, for at all these stops the people gathered to meet him, enthralled to think that a Governor would actually take the trouble to visit them. As an exercise in public relations the tour was a tremendous success; as a rest from official duties it could not have been a greater failure. But it was what he had wanted: he really had met the people, the ordinary, everyday people who were his constant concern.

On his return to Sydney the ceaseless round of State occasions and other engagements started again, and he was soon suggesting that every Governor should be granted an 8-hour day. His sister left for England in September, at the end of her leave of absence, and soon he was off again to the outback, this time to Cobar, Wilcannia and Broken Hill on his farthest border to the west with South Australia. In January, 1900 he visited Norfolk Island, the most eastern part of his territory far out in the Pacific Ocean, where he learned of Queen Victoria's death; in March he went north again, to Glen Innis and Inverell north of Sydney, where his tour came to an abrupt end when he learned of the death at Bloemfontein of his much-loved brother Eddie, who was serving with the Grenadier Guards in the Boer War. He returned at once to Sydney and cancelled all festivities for a period of mourning. He resumed this tour in June, visiting Tenterfield, Casino, Byron Bay, Murwillumba and Grafton, and in September his last visit was to Goulborn, south of Sydney, for a Church gathering.

He spent more time visiting outlying communities than any previous Governor had ever done. His recorded speeches are typically outspoken in their condemnation of 'sweated' labour and what he called 'sin and misery' in the big cities. At this time various areas of New South Wales were suffering from what is described as an unspecified 'plague', as well as exceptionally severe drought. He used his authority to enable ruthless measures to be taken, like the demolition of houses to counter epidemics—public health was always one of his greatest concerns—though some officials appear to have felt they should be beneath the notice of the Governor. As he had offended many on his arrival by a rather tactless quotation in his first speech, so he upset some when in a speech to the Sydney branch of the Christian Social Union he discussed Australian democracy and Australian complacency, concluding with the battle cry of 'We have got government of the people by the people and it is our business to see that the government is *for* the people'. But apparently some felt it was not the Governor's business.

He had been deeply concerned in the South African conflict since his arrival; there had been detailed discussions concerning the possible sending of an Australian contingent, which had finally been agreed, and it left Sydney on 30 October, 1899. He became personally involved in the arrangements for its despatch, and soon for the care of those who returned wounded. From now on he devoted a great deal of his time to visiting the troops; there were almost daily parades and inspections which the Governor was expected to attend, and about which he never complained. A second contingent was sent in January, 1900.

Yet, amidst all his comings and goings and his unconcealed satisfaction in his appointment not only as Governor but also after a few months as Colonel-in-Chief of the Australian Horse—an appointment he took very seriously—he never lost his interest in the 'ordinary folk', as he called them once. This is nowhere more evidenced than by the discovery of a few letters and cables, amongst all his official documents, concerning ways of improving the beef and dairy stock on local farms; for this purpose he finally donated and imported a prize-winning bull called 'Barrister' from his own herd at Madresfield.

The Confederation of the six Australian colonies had been under discussion for some years, and a draft constitution had been agreed and a referendum held in 1898, when only New South Wales had rejected it. Modifications had not long been accepted by all when Beauchamp's appointment was announced, and therefore on his arrival at Sydney he was pressed for his views on the subject. But if the Press hoped that his Excellency's inexperience would result in a newsworthy gaffe, they were disappointed. Indeed, Beauchamp's reply could hardly have been more diplomatic. He declared that he was personally an ardent federalist, but was not disposed to enter in any degree whatsoever into the controversy, since he understood that there was no disagreement regarding the principle; it was merely a question of terms, and that was 'a matter upon which the people themselves should be left to exercise their unfettered judgement'. In due course an amended constitution was accepted by all six colonies which would become the six states of the Confederation.

Whilst Governor of New South Wales, Beauchamp wrote privately to Joseph Chamberlain, the Prime Minister at the time, pleading for more consideration to be given to the salaries of Governors of smaller states; by his own account he had been somewhat startled when he found certain demands on his own expenditure; he was, for instance, expected to pay the salary of any aide-de-camp he felt he needed as well as other staff. There is no reply to his letter in the Madresfield archives but it is interesting that when his successor as Governor of New South Wales (Lord Hopetoun, later first Marquess of Linlithgow) resigned after two years, he gave as his reason the insufficiency of the salary.

From the outset it had been agreed that Beauchamp's appointment as Governor would end with the inauguration of the Federation. This date was now fixed for 1 January, 1901, but he decided that he would in fact leave Sydney on 1 November, 1900, justifying his early departure on the grounds that he had had no break from official duties since his arrival. Rather surprisingly, even those papers which had been most hostile since his arrival found something kind to say about him on his departure. Typical was the *Sydney Morning Herald*, which listed both his good and his bad deeds, and endeavoured to make amends for any share in his difficulties, commenting that 'every four years we receive from England a gentleman who, however sympathetic, is much in the dark as to our local lines of cleavage in politics and otherwise'. One unidentified newspaper commented that 'Although quite young, Lord Beauchamp has already shown considerable promise, in spite of the fact that his reign in New South Wales has not been altogether a success. The social aspect of Sydney would be difficult for any newcomer to understand, as there is a certain set whose members make it their proud boast to taboo Government House and who do not in any way acknowledge the Governor as a social power'. But a columnist in *The Bulletin* after commenting that he had managed to offend someone every time, no matter what he did, went on: 'And yet, all the time, everybody is perfectly well aware that never, never, never have we had a Gov. who has Tried So Hard to be a good Gov. all round, to please everybody—nobodies and somebodies—from Potts Point to Waterloo inclusive. Those in favour of the motion say aye! The ayes have it'.

There were many individuals who regretted his going and who kept in touch with him for a long time; in fact he visited the country twice in later years, once staying for six months. Many of his long-standing contacts were with the Church, especially with the diocese of Melanesia, and also many clerical friends—Madresfield subsequently had an Australian rector for several years; his concern for ex-soldiers, particularly the wounded, and the unemployed, was lasting and far-reaching.

He did not return directly from Australia to England, but took the opportunity to travel extensively in the Far East, gathering information on sociological conditions. However, he left no record of these travels apart from a number of personal photographs. When he visited America in the autumn of 1938, he intended to return via Australia where he had an engagement to broadcast on the situation in Europe—an appointment destined never to be kept.

His return to Worcestershire on 25 April 1901 was an extraordinary event. Escorted by mounted tenantry as he drove from the railway station at Malvern Link, his carriage passed through cheering crowds along the three miles to the entrance gate to the Court grounds, where a gold and green triumphal arch had been erected, surmounted by his coronet and crest in flowers with the Gaelic welcome *Céad mile fáilte* on a banner, which would have made his great-grandmother Catherine Denne smile rather wryly. There were flags innumerable and a guard of honour of the girls from the Industrial School, and then—the last evidence of serfdom in Madresfield—the horses were taken out and the carriage was drawn up the drive by estate employees to the front door, where a loyal address in an elaborate casket was presented.

It might have turned the head of any young man of 30 returning home after two years' absence, except that this young man had spent two years nominally in charge of a bustling, thriving colony that was already looking ahead to full self-government. The colony had firmly demonstrated to its erstwhile Governor that at the beginning of the 20th century, 18th-century uniforms and 19th-century mindsets were both unacceptable. Beauchamp tended to retain his affection for the uniforms, but his mind had already left the 19th century behind, and he now had no doubt as to his own motivation for the future: concern for the underdog.

The warmth of his welcome home was also calculated to remove the misgivings, if any remained, of the unsure young man who had faced the brash, critical onlookers as he had stepped ashore at Sydney two years previously. In the weeks immediately following his

The wedding of Earl Beauchamp and Lady Lettice Grosvenor

return, there was an outpouring of affection and encouragement from the whole county that helped to efface some of the more painful memories of official life Down Under. A rather surprising development was an avalanche of invitations from Anglican bishops and various societies to both Beauchamp and Lady Mary to address their gatherings on life in Australia, with particular regard to the conditions of the working classes. But there was one shadow. Members of his old college, Christ Church, wished to invite Beauchamp to honour him on his return. The dean refused permission unless Beauchamp first publicly apologised for his disobedience in attending the Blenheim Palace party, in defiance of the prohibition, more than ten years previously. As might have been expected, Beauchamp refused.

On 26 July, 1902, Beauchamp married Lady Lettice Grosvenor, sister of the second Duke of Westminster, who was destined to become known as one of the great Society hostesses of the 20th century. There is an interesting account in *Certain Delightful English Towns*, published in 1906, in which the American author, W.D. Howells (1837-1920), gives a stranger's reaction to the contemporary scene. Bored with Malvern, which he found 'so very, very pleasant, though so very, very dull', he went in desperate search of diversion to the recently-established show of the Madresfield Agricultural Society. This had been started as a means of both educating and encouraging the local tenants and farmers in good agricultural practice, though later it showed tendencies of becoming an outlet for the gentry to show off their

Lady Lettice Grosvenor

horses, the tenants and farmers their skills, and the lesser orders due respect for the established order. But it had many valuable aspects, and it survived until 1999, when it was put into, one hopes, temporary abeyance. However, in 1908 it was still a novel event, and probably some of the American's comments were unjustified. On the August Bank Holiday the author, overcome by boredom, noticed that Malvern:

> ... seemed the less reasoned resort of crowds of harmless young people, who perhaps thought they were seeing the world there, since it was the height of the Malvern season. They were at one time more definitely attracted by the Flower Show at the neighboring seat of a great nobleman, which was opened by his lady with due ceremonies, and which enjoyed a greater popular favor. I myself followed with the trippers there, partly because I had long read of that kind of English thing without seeing it, and because in the spacious leisure of Malvern it was difficult to invent occupations that would fill the time between luncheon and dinner, even with an hour out for an afternoon nap.
>
> It was just a pleasant drive to the nobleman's place, and my progress was attended by a sentiment of circus-day in the goers and comers on foot and in fly, and the loungers strewn on the grass of the roadsides and the open lots. At the gate of the nobleman's grounds, we paid a modest entrance, and there were still modester fees for several of the exhibits. One of these was a tent where under a strong magnifying-glass a community of ants were offering their peculiar domestic and social economy to the study of the curious. But, if I rightly remember, the pavilion which sheltered the flower-show was free to all who could walk through its sultry air without stifling; it was really not so much a show of flowers as of fruits and vegetables, which indeed bore the heat better. Another free performance was the rivalry, apparently of amateurs, in simple feats of carpentry and joiner-work as applied to fence building; but this was of a didactic effect from which it was a relief to turn to the idle and useless adventures of the people who lost themselves in a maze, or labyrinthine hedge, and shared the innocent hilarity of the spectators watching their bewilderment from a high ground hard by. All the time there was a band playing [probably under the baton of Frank, or his brother Edward, Elgar] which when it played a certain familiar rag-time measure was loudly applauded and forced to play it again and again. It was a proud moment for the exile from a country whose black step-children had contributed these novel motives to the world's music, in the intervals of being lynched.
>
> The scene was all very familiar and very strange, with qualities of a subdued county fair at home, but more ordered and directed than such things are with us. As I say, I had long known its like in literature, and I was now glad to find it so realistic. My pleasure in it overflowed when the nobleman who had lent his premises for the show, came walking out among the people, bare-headed, in a suit of summer gray, with his lady beside him, and paused to speak, amid the general emotion, with a neat old woman of humble class, whose hand his lady had shaken. That, I said to myself, was quite as it should be in its allegiance to immemorial tradition and its fidelity to fiction; it could have formed the initial moment of a hundred thousand English novels. If it could not have formed a like moment in American romance, it is because our millionaires, in their shyness of subpoenas or of interviews, do not yet open their private

grounds for flower-shows. It needs many centuries to mellow the conditions for the effect I had witnessed, and we must not be impatient.

The lord and his lady had come out of a mansion that did not look very mediaeval, though it had a moat round it, with ducks in the moat, and in the way to its portal a force of footmen to confirm any comer in his misgiving that the house was closed to the public, and to direct him to the pleasance beyond. This was a lawned and gardened place, enclosed with a green wall of hedge, and guarded on one side with a succession of pedestals bearing classic busts [now known as the Caesars' Lawn]. It was charming in the afternoon sun, with groups of people seriously, if somewhat awe-strickenly, enjoying themselves. The inferiors in England never take that ironical attitude towards their superiors which must long delay a real classification of society with us. When there one accepts the situation, and becomes at least gentry if one can, with all the assumptions and responsibilities which station implies.

Yes, possibly Madresfield deserved censure for its perceived snobbery at that time. This onlooker's account is of one of the early agricultural shows, and may be the first which the earl and his bride attended. Countess Lettice Beauchamp died in July 1936, and was buried at her ancestral home near Chester.

The Politician
The political life of the seventh earl has received scant evaluation from historians, yet at the height of his career he was a man of influence within the innermost circle of Government, though not infrequently at odds with the Establishment.

After his return to England from Australia in 1901, Beauchamp gave himself wholly to the work of politics, both in the House of Lords as a member of the Liberal Party and also a most enthusiastic Free Trader and a Radical. He was just 30 years old, young enough for it to be said of him that he had 'an impish spirit of mischief which has caused him to be described as the Lloyd George of the House of Lords', but he was never accused of being devious or insincere. No longer inexperienced, he returned to a House of Lords where it must have seemed to him that the kind of politicking with which he had had to deal in what he had regarded as only a newly developing colony, was in fact the only kind that his own countrymen knew. In a man so devoted to the memory of his father, it must have needed some deep conviction to turn against his father's conservatism. The seeds had been sown in his youth by perhaps the most unlikely hands. His mother, whom he had barely known but whom he nevertheless placed on a pedestal, had had a deep and genuine concern for the less privileged, evidenced not only by her introduction into sleepy, rural Madresfield of an Industrial School for orphaned or otherwise abandoned young girls, but possibly also by accounts of her early attempts at welfare work in the slums of Newcastle before she met Frederick Lygon; the Oxford Mission which had taken him as an undergraduate to the East End of London, and his contacts with the Salvation Army; his experiences in visiting the isolated miners in the Australian outback; his interest both in Australia and in England in the deprived inner city areas—all these strands had combined to develop a concern for the underprivileged wherever they were to be found.

His first speech in the House of Lords, in 1902, was on the subject of education, perhaps not surprisingly, for he had inherited his father's enthusiasm for opening the doors of learning to as many people as possible. But he developed other crusades, and within a few years was a notable speaker on a number of subjects. These included Public Health; Education at every level; Free Trade and Tariff Reform; Foreign Affairs, especially South Africa and the Boer War and its aftermath, and then the Congo Reform Association. But there were many other concerns. He became Chairman of the Church of England Liberal and Progressive Union. By the General Election of November, 1905— the first in which he took an active part—he was speaking in support of Liberal candidates all over England. Although he was not offered any post in the Government following the Liberal victory, he was asked to undertake Home Office work in the Lords, and he agreed. Soon his services were in great demand. Apart from Home Office matters, he also agreed to other M.P.s' requests for support by way of speeches on such matters as justices of the peace, police superannuation, juvenile smoking, and workmen's compensation. In the following year the list lengthens: vivisection, coal mines (Eight Hours), court of criminal appeal, state reformatories, probation, released persons (Poor Law Relief), regulation of advertisements, marriages (Provisional Order), metropolitan police, London traffic, historical manuscripts, white phosphorus marches prohibition, employment of women (laundries), plural voting, education (England and Wales), and cabs (fares). Typical is a letter from the London Cabdrivers' Trade Union dated 31 August, 1907, thanking him 'for the brilliant manner in which you presented the Bill on Cabs and Omnibuses'. By 1907 he was treasurer of the Anti-Sweating League (as against sweated labour) among whose Vice-Presidents were Keir Hardie, Sidney and Beatrice Webb, and H.G. Wells. Somewhat ironically, it is in this year that he also followed in his father's footsteps as Lord Steward of the Royal Household.

The list of Bills with whose passage through the Lords he was closely connected continues in 1908 with those on weekly rest days, polling districts, incest, endowed schools (Masters), municipal representation, borough funds, wild birds and children— this last being especially significant since it set up juvenile courts and at last abolished the sentencing of children to prison.

Equally important, as he was now a front bench spokesman on Ireland, he made two major speeches in 1913 and two in 1914, for as late as July, 1914, the British Government seem to have been more occupied

Sketch of the earl in c.1904

with what they thought of as a purely internal matter between the Imperial power and one of its colonies, whilst failing to realise fully the import of developments on the Continent.

Vehemently opposed by the Conservatives, the proposal had already led to the emergence of Edward Carson (who coined the phrase 'No surrender'), leader of the Ulster Unionists' open defiance of the supremacy of the Government. On 29 January, 1913, Beauchamp made a speech in the House of Lords which had a considerable impact outside Parliament. It illustrated not only his grasp of the situation as it was, but of the factors which had led to it and of the possible outcome if Home Rule was not granted. He started by recalling how at least Gladstone's Bill, which he had been 'dragged from somewhat fruitless studies at Oxford' to vote against, had discussed the question of entitlement to self-government. The Bill with which they were now dealing dealt only with how that should be implemented. He drew on examples throughout the Commonwealth where the inhabitants of countries had been granted self-determination, and emphasised that it was only a small minority in the whole of Ireland that opposed the grant of Home Rule to the rest. He spoke of the unwavering resistance of the Irish people to British rule through many centuries; of the misconception in England that most of the Irish were merely peasant farmers, at best, and that there was a similarly clear-cut distinction between the two main religions. But in particular he referred to 'the small minority in one corner of Ireland who persuade your Lordships to refuse to the rest of Ireland what four-fifths of her people want. We say that such a claim is an intolerable claim ...' He was adamant that Carson's opposition was based purely on religious prejudice. 'There are twenty-eight Parliaments, I believe, within the British Empire, and noble Lords opposite wish us to believe that the twenty-ninth will work destruction to the whole Imperial system ... We are anxious that [the Irish] should have the same privilege which we have ourselves ...' He castigated the occasional English visitor to Ireland who 'after a weekend or two ... tells us that the House of Lords knows far better what is the real wish of the Irish peasant ...' But perhaps what most incensed his Conservative opponents was when he added that:

> They tell us that the character of the Irish is fickle, and that it is only in this country that you can find consistent politics. Surely the facts are exactly contrary to that. We are amongst the most fickle people in matters of our ordinary politics. Almost on every occasion the people change their rulers, and it requires either the crisis of a great war, such as that in 1900, or a great constitutional mistake, as in 1909, to make the people of this country renew their confidence for a second time in those who have governed them during the past few years. We change, but not Ireland. From the time when O'Connell spoke of repeal ... Ireland has asked for the right to manage her own affairs. Whatever has happened, nothing has confused the issue in Ireland.

He attacked how 'what could be done has been done to drive the people from the soil of Ireland' and listed how other rights such as the franchise had eventually been granted only with great reluctance. Again and again he referred to the small minority who were now obstructing Home Rule, and he concluded with an onslaught upon those who were supporting Edward Carson in his declared defiance:

> In 1893 noble Lords opposite brought down upon the supporters of the Bill charges of sedition, disloyalty, and lawlessness. Now we find that it is the allies of noble Lords opposite who have refused to discountenance disorder in Belfast ...

At this time officers in the British Army stationed at The Curragh (near Dublin) had mutinied and refused to bear arms against Carson's supporters in the Six Counties, and Beauchamp's words could not have been more unwelcome to the Unionists. Already angered by his 'desertion', as they saw it, to the Liberals, this speech gave them an opening for the vilification which was increased when he later became an outspoken advocate for negotiations to avoid hostilities in the international arena and then for peace to limit the damage of a prolonged war. It had been rumoured, on his return from Australia, that he was about to be offered the Governor-Generalship of Ireland. Perhaps the rumour had been inspired by the reports in many newspapers of his success with the disaffected miners in the Australian outback; certainly wherever he had gone he had been enthusiastically received. That those miners were not naive was illustrated by one who commented to an English newspaper that 'He's a decent man and he'll shake hands with anybody', to which another added 'Though he always looks first to see if your hand's been properly washed'. It is tempting now, a century later, to wonder how the despised Irish might have reacted, and whether this also was not a missed golden opportunity. Would Catherine Denne's great-grandson have succeeded where everyone else has failed? It is certainly very difficult to visualise any contemporary politician, peer or commoner, daring to express Beauchamp's opinions even now.

It is a long and complicated task to follow the various shifts of opinion amongst those involved as the prospect of war loomed ever nearer in the weeks of June and July, 1914. On Sunday, 3 August, 1914, Great Britain declared war with Germany; only one Cabinet minister was available to sign as a witness to the declaration by George V—Beauchamp, already known as an earnest worker for peace. At a subsequent Cabinet meeting on the same day Beauchamp tendered his resignation; at another Cabinet meeting that evening Asquith persuaded him to withdraw it, and late that night Beauchamp wrote his own account of the affair, in which he frankly admitted that they had all agreed on 'a form of words - we were all jaded and exhausted. I cannot but feel that our promise to France [to defend her coast and shipping against Germany, a promise he had always opposed] is a *casus belli* to Germany. Alas for this country.' Asquith's acknowledgement of the withdrawal of his resignation was written in a few pencilled words: 'I cannot say how much it means to me to have you still by my side. L.A.'

Beauchamp had numerous messages of support. To one friend he wrote the following day about the pressure he felt Asquith had exerted:

> I am chiefly conscious through all this strain of the appeals to one's loyalty to the party. It seems so presumptuous to set up my own opinion against that of one to whom I owe so much allegiance as the Prime Minister. To me he is the chief figure in my political life. Always kind and considerate, how difficult to resist a personal appeal.

But from now on it would seem that Beauchamp was increasingly sidelined by Asquith himself. Various important Bills, including that for Home Rule in Ireland, were suspended for the duration of the war, and when in May, 1915, Asquith reshuffled his Cabinet he found no place for Beauchamp, and Beauchamp never again held a post in Government. Again there were numerous letters of support; one from Edmund Gosse the poet is typical:

> This is a good moment, perhaps, to remind you, as I really have no need to remind myself, how solid and broad is the political position you have built up for yourself in the last six or seven years ... No one of your age has done so much in the time.

Beauchamp's main focus was now concentrated on free trade, which was increasingly identified with a campaign for a negotiated peace with Germany. He became President of the Free Trade Union in 1915; founded in 1903, its membership consisted largely of businessmen and economists as well as politicians campaigning for free trade as opposed to protectionism. Henceforth Beauchamp to a great extent shunned the House of Lords as his platform.

Then, on 31 November, 1917, the *Daily Telegraph* published a letter from the fifth Marquess of Lansdowne. As a Conservative, he had been leader of his party in the House of Lords in 1903, but had become increasingly critical of its policies, and publication of this letter brought him almost united condemnation from his colleagues. This is not the place to go deeply into the matter, but he was one of many who believed that although the Allies should not weaken in their determination to win the war 'its prolongation will spell ruin for the civilized world ... What will be the value of the blessings of peace to nations so exhausted that they can hardly stretch out a hand with which to grasp them?' He felt that the Government had misrepresented their aims as the total annihilation of Germany, and he outlined five proposals which he believed could lead to peaceful coexistence.

It is clear from correspondence in the Madresfield archives that Lansdowne and Beauchamp had corresponded on the subject before the letter's publication. Its appearance produced a sensational response from both opponents and supporters. One of the first letters in support came from Beauchamp and was printed in the *Manchester Guardian* of 5 December, citing the positive effects of the Austro-Prussian war of 1870 and the negative outcome of the Franco-Prussian war of 1870 to illustrate his argument that magnanimity in victory would be an asset rather than a liability.

The furore caused by 'the Lansdowne letter', as it came to be known, continued into 1918, even though the Official Press Bureau, invoking powers under the Defence of the Realm Act, banned its release in pamphlet form; the publication of pacifist or dissenting beliefs was already virtually impossible. A series of public meetings in various centres followed, at most of which Beauchamp was present and spoke. However, following a meeting in Birmingham which although very well attended had been described as 'private', a move was made to ask the government to suppress all public expression of pacifist views. Beauchamp's reply was that the meeting had been designated as 'private' because the German spring offensive was then at its height and he wished 'to avoid giving any sign or appearance of disunion in our ranks at home'.

That complaint went no further, and the arguments and the meetings dragged on throughout that summer until the final meeting in London in October. The end of the war was now in sight, and in a newspaper interview of the time Beauchamp showed his anxiety about what kind of peace lay ahead:

> It is very important that while an armistice should ensure that the position of the Allies can in no possible way be worse at its conclusion, the terms should not be so humiliating as to allow the Pan-Germans to rally opinion in favour of the continuance of the war as a war of defence. It is easier to go to war than it is to conclude peace ...

Since the beginning of 1918, Beauchamp had taken advantage of his release from any Government appointment to intervene as he chose, whenever he disagreed with alterations to various constitutional matters. He spoke on the Representation of the People Bill and in May he introduced a Sexual Offences Bill which included a provision that the transgressions of both sexes should be dealt with on a basis of equality. In June he moved all the stages of a Bill enabling women to become Justices of the Peace. He worked tirelessly on behalf of conscientious objectors, as indeed he had done through the war years. He had become a supporter of the Union of Democratic Control, which the Home Secretary had tried unsuccessfully to get classified as a subversive organisation, though Beauchamp apparently rejected a move to make him its leader. He moved the Sex Disqualification (Removal) Bill in July, 1919. But by far the greater bulk of his correspondence at this time shows him to have been immersed in working for the Free Trade Union.

His political stance continued to offend the traditionalists; he said himself on one occasion that:

> Liberals had been blamed for the fact that there was a Labour government in office. He confessed that he was wholly impenitent in regard to that matter ... It was evident that the Labour Government would depend a great deal on the support of the Liberal Party in the House of Commons and he hoped that support would be given to no stinted extent.

But at last it seemed that he had been reinstated in favour when on the retirement of Earl Grey in 1924 he was chosen as Leader of the Liberals in the House of Lords. 'No better choice could be found than in Lord Beauchamp ... who is known to possess those qualities of tact and personal charm which, equally with his stock of personal acumen and his alertness in debate, are essential to every successful leader' wrote one journalist, and another opined that 'he is quite the most active and regular of the Liberal Peers at Westminster and it is largely due to his influence that the Liberal peers agreed, months before Liberal reunion came, to act under one leadership and to forget the division of the Coalition period'. There were similar complimentary references in other newspapers which Beauchamp and his family kept. However, they had an unfortunate habit of omit-

William Rankin's painting in 1924 celebrating the 21st birthday of Viscount Elmley, later to become the eighth earl

ting the name and date of almost every source of these cuttings, now so carefully preserved in his scrapbooks at Madresfield. But omens for his success as Liberal leader in the House of Lords were not good. The party was now almost terminally divided by internal differences and also because Grey, tired after a long career in politics, had lost his enthusiasm for Parliamentary work. It was a thankless task which was passed on to Beauchamp. He continued the struggle to reunite the Party; as was his wont, he devoted himself entirely to efforts to reconcile the various contentious elements, but he met with no success, and eventually he seems, not to have abandoned his endeavours but to have allowed himself at last to develop the other talents with which he had been endowed. But he did not desert his politics, as witness the burning of his effigy by local Young Conservatives in Worcestershire, their retaliation for one of his forthright speeches on free trade.

Beauchamp had a very high regard for the responsibilities laid on him by his inheritance of wealth and privilege, and he accepted many official appointments and honours as the years passed: Member of the Privy Council in 1906, Captain of the Corps of Gentlemen-at-Arms 1906-7, Lord Steward to the Royal Household 1907-10—an office he especially valued because his father, along with a very distant ancestor, had held the post—Lord President of the Council in 1910 and again in 1914-15, and First Commissioner of Works 1910-14. He had been created KCMG in 1899 and, most importantly from his point of view as it was the premier order of chivalry and had enormous historic value, a Knight of the Garter in 1914. In 1911 he was appointed Lord Lieutenant of Gloucestershire, a traditional appointment for the Lygons, and in 1913 Lord Warden of the Cinque Ports.

He was elected as Chancellor of the University of London in 1929, and perhaps his last major speech was made on the occasion of his installation on 22 November in that year. After thanking Convocation for the honour, and the Senate for the degree —'a unique honour' he called it—bestowed upon him (did Oxford's reject find particular pleasure in that?) he went on to mention his own entry into public life as:

> a member of the London School Board it seems somehow appropriate that, having almost begun my public life on a body which dealt with Elementary Education, I should find myself now associated with the University of London. The University is, perhaps, the largest University in the world. It has a vast student body who ... are realising more and more their unity in diversity ...,

and he went on to contrast this university, founded only in 1836

> when the ancient universities were not open to all comers, to hold forth to all classes and denominations without any distinction whatsoever an encouragement for pursuing ... education. It imposed no test on opinions, religious or political. It was the first English university to open its doors to women. It has always mentioned the poor students and made easy their access to a degree, and in the present day it yields to no other University in the facilities which it offers to those poorer men and women who come to it ...

After quoting figures to illustrate its enormous growth in numbers since 1914, he went on to claim that

> It is, therefore, a well-founded claim that the University of London is easily the largest university in the Empire, if not indeed in the world ... let me express my admiration for those whose desire for knowledge is so great that, having worked all day in order to earn a daily or a weekly wage, spend their evenings preparing for their examination ... At a time when universities were becoming more and more the playground of the rich, London University came into existence as an intellectual treasure house for the poor. Though it must inevitably cater more and more for those men and women who can make their studies a full-time occupation, let us never forget the needs of those who cannot afford to do so...

However, Beauchamp's own political activities had already lessened. After the death of Lord Lansdowne in 1927, he attempted to reconcile the Asquith and Lloyd George factions in the Liberal Party, though with only limited success, and gradually he withdrew from the political front line.

The Artist
Beauchamp was a highly gifted man, and it is perhaps a matter for regret that he allowed political arguments to deflect him from what might well have been a distinguished artistic career. After the victory of the Liberals in the second election of 1910, Beauchamp was made First Commissioner of Works, and in this appointment, for perhaps the only time, he managed to combine his political work with his artistic instincts—he undertook and completed a major re-arrangement of the works of art in the Palace of Westminster, for which he was widely praised.

However, he had been interested in the Arts and Crafts Movement since its development, and in 1902 his bride proposed as her wedding gift to him the ornate decora-

Paintings on the walls of the chapel depicting the earl's children. The child on the left is Richard Lygon, the earl's third son and father of Lady Morrison, current owner of the Court

tion by Henry Payne of the simple chapel at Madresfield Court. The work, scheduled to take a comparatively short space of time, was spread over a number of years and also extended to work elsewhere in the house. The chapel was primarily Payne's design—he had already been asked to provide stained glass windows, but Beauchamp took a decisive interest in every aspect. The decoration was carried out by staff and students of the Birmingham Municipal School of Art & Design (the 'Birmingham Group') and is still regarded as a masterpiece of the Arts and Crafts Movement, recently restored to its former glory. Beauchamp also chose the inscription for the altar frontal, which is not strictly (as is often incorrectly stated) cloth-of-gold, but a form of embroidery known as 'or nué', now rarely seen because of its expense, except in museums. The embroidery was made under the direction of his sister Lady Mary. He also supervised the design of the chalice and paten which were produced by the Birmingham Group.

But one feature of the whole project has almost invariably been overlooked ever since its installation. Outside the chapel, above the stone steps leading down to the lower floor where the altar frontals were stored, Beauchamp installed a stained glass window of his own design, overlooking the moat. At first glance it appears to be only an illustration of the story, in St. Matthew, chapter 8, of the Roman centurion who begged Christ to heal his servant, but did not expect Christ to visit his home for that purpose since, he said humbly, 'I am not worthy that thou shouldest come under my roof'. The stained glass window that the earl designed tells more than that.

The top of the window is filled by the arms of Lygon and Grosvenor, his wife's family. Beneath, a lady is shown in a bed, apparently at the moment of death. Beside the bed stands a young girl, holding her younger brother by the hand whilst they grieve. One is reminded that the earl had lost his mother when he was only three, and it was his elder sister to whom he henceforth turned for guidance. Then there is a grass space enclosing within a wooden fence five lambs; when as a boy the earl had been asked if he would like a place in the grounds to design his own garden, he had asked for a space with a wooden fence around it 'like the Saxons would have had'. When the window was made the earl had a family of only five children (two more

The new Kempley Church in 1903

arrived later), hence there are only five lambs safe within the fence. Next comes the most important part of the whole picture. The centurion kneels before Christ. But this Christ is not a typical Edwardian blue-eyed, blond figure, but a Christ whose dark brown hair is already showing signs of gray, as Beauchamp's own father must have appeared for most of his heir's life. The centurion is an unmistakable self-portrait, which Payne praised for its success in a venture where many artists fail. It is indeed the seventh earl dressed in Roman costume, but the sword he is offering to Christ as a sign of allegiance is in fact the Sword of State which the young Earl Beauchamp had borne so proudly at the coronation of George V in 1911. The verse 'Lord, I am not worthy that thou shouldest come under my roof ...' so well-known to Christians because of its frequent use before receiving

Communion, has in this instance an added poignancy, for this window, the earl's most personal material contribution to the whole project, is outside the ornate chapel.

Beauchamp also spent much time choosing and designing a studio for himself at the time the central staircase hall of the Court was being altered. Eventually he found a suitable space on the first floor, though its exact position is now difficult to determine. Here he was at last able to indulge his interest in sculpture, and here he produced perhaps his finest piece, *The Golfer*, which may still be seen in the smoking room, although sadly it has now lost its miniature club. This nude figure, in the typical position of raising his club as he concentrates on his shot, was exhibited in the Paris Exhibition in 1920 and very widely acclaimed, not only for its execution but for the perfection of detail in the portrayal of an exceptionally difficult pose.

Shortly after his marriage he had undertaken a perhaps more ambitious project, when he decided to provide a new parish church for Kempley on one of his Gloucestershire landholdings. The very ancient church, whilst deserving conservation—which he assisted in providing—was not well placed for modern needs, and he offered a site at the other end of the village. Here in due course was built the Church of St. Edward to Beauchamp's own design, and all the materials used, so far as practicable, came from local Beauchamp-owned resources. For instance, the massive oak timber used in the construction of the roof was felled and converted in the parish under the supervision of Madresfield's head forester. However, the consecration was the occasion of some acrimonious correspondence with the bishop of Gloucester. Lady Beauchamp, whose birthday was on Christmas Day, insisted that that should be the date of the ceremony; the bishop was adamant that that would be improper since no event other than the birth of Christ could be celebrated on 25 December. Eventually a compromise was reached when the bishop agreed to consecrate the church on St. Stephen's Day (26 December). Then there was another hitch because at a very late moment in the proceedings the diocesan authorities objected to the presence of the conventional figures on the rood. These were hurriedly removed, and apparently stored in a nearby barn until they were reinstated, with no recorded objection, some 40 years later.

Another example of his excursion into architecture was in the building of four cottages at Madresfield (Nos. 19-22.) The cost of construction was minimal and the cottages were recommended as an example to other landowners as being both useful and economical, but they were not universally popular with their occupants and were rather unattractive. Beauchamp's heir commented that from the date of their building they had always been known as 'the ugly four'.

The End

Although as already mentioned Beauchamp had begun to withdraw from public life, he still retained a number of official posts which made comparatively little demand upon his energies. His health was no longer robust—it is believed that he had developed cancer, and his heart was giving cause for anxiety—but he must also have been disheartened by the failure of all his efforts to reunite the divided factions of the Liberal party. In addition, he had made many enemies amongst what was called 'his own class' by his acknowledged leanings towards left of centre politics. That one of the wealthiest of that class, the latest head of a family who traced its ancestry back over more centuries than could most of its rivals, should so betray their claim to dominance on the grounds of heredity, was, to some, unforgivable.

In May, 1931, Beauchamp tendered his resignation on health grounds. By return, Lloyd George replied:

My dear Beauchamp,

I am very grieved to hear from your Doctor that you are suffering from cardiac fatigue, and that a period of comparative rest is essential to your recovery. Your partial and temporary retirement from the very hard work you have done for us will be a real loss to the Party. We have come to rely so much upon your ready and very effective help in all our difficulties, that we shall miss it more than I can tell you. However, I hope that you will consider your health as first and foremost, so that you may have a full chance of an early restoration to complete vigour.

The responsibilities of the Party are growing, and therefore its anxieties. The Government are relying more and more upon our counsel and co-operation. I dare not think what we should have done had your loyal service not been available to us during the last trying few years, but they will be needed as much, if not more than ever, in the coming months.

With best wishes, believe me,
Ever sincerely,
D. Lloyd George

Two years ago accounts were found at Madresfield which corroborate his illness and payments to his doctor in connection with medical visits to his London home at this time.

That hope of a return to Parliament and Party was never fulfilled. Beauchamp spent his few remaining years, at first recuperating on the Riviera, usually accompanied by one or two of his children, and then in 1936 returning with the hope that he would resume living permanently at Madresfield. But he had gone to America to fulfil a long-standing speaking engagement with the Ligon Family Association (an organisation of people bearing the Ligon surname, with its 15th century spelling, who claim origination from Madresfield), when he collapsed and died in New York on 10 November, 1938. He was brought home to be buried at the family home with his immediate forbears, in a village which had known and loved him as a friend first and an employer and landlord second.

His life as a statesman still waits for assessment by a competent biographer; this was a man who has never received from an unprejudiced commentator a full appraisal of not only perhaps his failings, but also, and far more important, his constant adherence to sincerely held convictions which, though unpopular in his lifetime, underpinned many years of public service, and which were far ahead of their time.

CHAPTER TWELVE
William, Eighth Earl Beauchamp (1903-1979)

William, the first child of the seventh Earl Beauchamp and Lady Lettice Grosvenor, was born on 3rd July, 1903. He was educated at Eton and then went on to Magdalen College at Oxford, so breaking the centuries-old Lygon connection with Christ Church. After university he became a second lieutenant in the 100th (Worcester and Oxford Yeomanry) Field Brigade, in 1922. Two years later he transferred to the Royal Tank Corps, with which he remained for the next four years.

He then went on a world tour, which was inspired by a desire to see Australia where his father had been Governor of New South Wales, New Zealand, India and later America and Canada. Following this, Viscount Elmley, as he was then, embarked on a political career by winning in 1929 the Conservative seat of Norfolk East for the Liberals, a seat which he retained, despite his subsequent change of party. After a short period with the National Liberals as an assistant Whip, he transferred his political allegiance to the Conservative Party, a change which caused some distress to his father. He retained the seat of Norfolk East until he resigned in 1938 on the death of his father and when he inherited the title.

Later he became Parliamentary Private Secretary to Mr. (later Lord) Hore Belisha, who held a variety of posts: Parliamentary Secretary to the Board of Trade, Financial Secretary to the Treasury, Minister of Transport and Secretary of State for War 1937-1938. Hore-Belisha became a valued friend of Viscount Elmley, but when the seventh Earl Beauchamp died, the new earl decided to devote his attention to his role as the owner of Madresfield, and moved into residence at his ancestral home.

He served during the 1939-1945 war as a captain in the R.A.O.C., but he left no record of his experiences during this time except for noting the extraordinary complications caused by the difficulties of his men to grasp the correct pronunciation of his name, which ranged from 'Bowkamp' to 'Bowshawm'.

The earl was especially pleased when it was decided that should it be considered necessary for the Royal Family to be evacuated from London, they would come to

Madresfield Court, and two bedrooms were kept prepared for the two princesses, Elizabeth and Margaret. As long as this provision was maintained, Lord Beauchamp on the occasion of each princess's birthday would leave at her bedside a new book, more appropriate to her age each year. It was possibly fortunate, for more than one reason, that it was never necessary to evacuate the royal children from London, for the room chosen as a suitable shelter in case Madresfield Court was bombed, was a tiny storeroom partially below the level of the moat, with two extremely narrow and barred windows which would not have allowed the escape of anyone in the event of fire.

After the war, when Madresfield Court became his permanent residence, the earl was involved with an increasing number of local organisations. In 1941 he was elected President of the Worcestershire Conservative Association. He was also elected to various other bodies: the Worcestershire branch—of which he was President for 24 years—of the Country Landowners Association, Worcestershire County Council, the Three Counties Agricultural Society—the focus of his interests becoming centred on the county in which his family's roots were so deep and long established. He had also served as a Justice of the Peace for over 30 years when he retired from the Bench in 1973.

The eighth earl was undoubtedly anxious to fulfil the obligations arising from his heritage, but to many he gave the impression of being an extremely reserved man who found it somewhat difficult to communicate easily with those outside his own very close circle. Yet behind the formal façade there was a kindly and conscientious human being who really cared about every facet of his heritage. This can be illustrated by two instances which show aspects of his character which were too little appreciated in his lifetime:

One retired employee remembers being introduced to him in 1966 in the library at the Court, when in a simple statement he revealed far more of his character than he probably realised:

> People ask me if living here amongst all these antiques and treasures is not rather like living in a museum, but my answer is that when I look at all these beautiful things I am reminded they were brought here by my ancestors, and so I am in fact surrounded by mementoes of my family. And I like to think that for 800 years this place has been owned by the same family, and it has always been the rule here that even the lowliest servant, right down to the latest vegetable maid in the kitchen, in fact anyone who feels aggrieved, has the right to complain direct to the Head of the Family himself. And now I am the Head of the Family, and I hope you will feel able to come direct to me if you need to do so.

So much for his attitude to his employees; he was never harsh in his treatment, and never knowingly allowed his name to be used in any way inconsistent with his character.

His attitude towards his heritage was well indicated by a broadcast which he made for the BBC Midlands Region in 1950, when he spoke about his beloved Madresfield—'my house' as he described it:

> It is completely surrounded by a moat 20 feet wide, happily now no longer necessary for defence. It contains some large carp who show themselves on sunny days, and

occasionally one sees the blue flash of a passing kingfisher ... We have a rock garden, a yew maze which I personally think is much better than Hampton Court, and a wonderful variety of trees and flowering shrubs. I enjoy the gardens most in April when they are carpeted with daffodils, narcissi, jonquils, tiger lilies and fritillaries ...

It is true that the gardens undoubtedly gave him much pleasure, but it was in his library, with its thousands of volumes, that he regularly sat, surrounded by books which he reckoned as his friends. He went on to list some more of the house's treasures, and his conclusion is significant: 'These are just a few of the many lovely things at Madresfield. I believe it is a house England can be proud of, and to keep it so is my greatest ambition.'

He had not really been prominent in public life, but those who knew him trusted him and respected him very highly. He died on 3 January, 1979, after a very long illness, and is buried at Madresfield. With his death the title of 'Beauchamp of Powyke' became extinct, for he had no children and there was no male member of the Lygon line to perpetuate the name so long associated with Madresfield Court. His death was truly the end of an era.

The earl had married in 1936, Fru Else Domonville de la Cour, daughter of an officer in the Danish navy and widow of a property developer. She was very active in many county concerns, particularly in connection with the St. John Ambulance Brigade, being the Worcester county president for 29 years, and she was made a Dame of the Order in 1957. During World War II she was closely connected with the organisation of the Women's Voluntary Service in Worcestershire, for which she later received the M.B.E. She also formed a Red Cross detachment in Malvern, and later became President of Worcestershire Girl Guides Association and was a strong supporter of the Women's Institute.

Long after the war she continued to take a keen interest in all these organisations and in local matters generally. It was she who introduced Malvern to the custom of having an illuminated Christmas tree (still continued), which during her lifetime was placed on Belle Vue Terrace. With her gift for organisation, and her striking personality, she was greatly in demand from a number of charities which benefitted from her patronage. She sustained her interest in all these organisations for many years, until she felt that age prevented her from taking as active a part as she would have wished.

In her younger years she had travelled extensively and spoke a number of languages. She was fluent in Danish and English, of course, but she also had a good command of French and Italian, and she continued to travel abroad each year for almost all her remaining years after her husband's death. She died in 1989, at the age of 94.

No one who met her ever forgot the experience, whether it was an informal encounter when she was riding her tricycle around the grounds of the Court, or on a formal occasion. In either case it was equally likely that she would be wearing an abundance of jewellery and smoking one of her small cigars. But Lady Beauchamp will be remembered by many for unexpected kindnesses, and more generally by the people of Malvern town. Some years older than her husband, she showed her devotion to him by helping to nurse him during his long final illness.

Both the earl and Lady Beauchamp are buried in the place they had chosen—on the site of the ancient church of Madresfield, near to the front entrance of the Court, and in the shadow of the Celtic cross which was erected in memory of the sixth Earl Beauchamp. It is entirely fitting that the last male representative of the Beauchamp connection should rest where seven centuries before, his ancestress Anne Beauchamp had built a little chapel for her family and its workers to worship. Surely no more appropriate place could have been chosen to lay to rest the last of both the Beauchamp of Powyke and of the Lygon lines.

Bibliography

Dangerfield, Geo. *The Strange Death of Liberal England* (1997)
FitzGibbon, Constantine *The Irish in Ireland* (1983)
Gaut, R.C. *History of Worcestershire Agriculture* (1939)
Howells, W.D. *Certain Delightful English Towns* (1906)
Jenkins of Hillhead *Learning the Lessons of History* (1991)
Joyce, Peter (ed.) *Towards the Sound of Gunfire!* (1994)
Mackay, H.F.B. *Saints and Leaders* (1928)
Madresfield Agricultural Society Quarterly magazine, vols.1-8 (1901-1908)
Morton, H.V. *In Search of Ireland* (1939)
Noakes, John Various publications 1851-1877
Smith, Brian S. *A History of Malvern* (1978)
Smith, Fr. Joseph, *Paul Mary Pakenham, Passionist* (1915, reprinted 1930)
Southall, Mary *A description of Malvern* (1822)
Trevelyan, G.M. *English Social History* (1948)
Willis-Bund, J.W. (ed.) *Victoria County History: Worcestershire* (1913)
Wilson, Joan *A Soldier's Wife: Wellington's Marriage* (1987)
Worcester Historical Society Various transcripts and registers

Index

Albert, Prince 80
Anglo-Saxons 1
Antoinette, Marie 29
Arle Court 7, 8
Arnold, Jarvis 43, 45-8, 56
Arts and Crafts Movement 116-7
Aston, Captain 11
Asquith 112, 116
Australia 102-6

Beauchamp, Alice 6
    Ann 3, 5, 6
    John 5, 6
    Richard 6
    Walter 6
Beauchamps of Powyke 5
    of Warwick 5
Belisha, Hoare 121
Belloc, Hillaire 102
Benson, E.F., Archbishop 83, 83
Biddulph, Francis 21
Birmingham Group, the 117
Bloomfield, Sir Benjamin 28, 31
Boer War 104
Bracy, de, Isabel 4
    Joan 4
    Sir Robert 3
    Wiliam 4
Braci, de 2
Braye, Catherine 52
Bridges, Elizabeth 14
Bull, Edward 11-12

Carlisle 37
Caroline, Princess 43
Carson, Edward 111
Cavendish, Charles 64-5
Chamberlain, Joseph 102
Church affairs 7, 8-9, 81-7
Civil War 11, 13
Clonmell, Lord 50
Cocks, Margaret 17
Corbyn, Margaret 15-16
    Thomas 15
Cornish Music Festival 98
Cotton, Sir Willoughby 53
Cour, Fru Else de la 123
Court of Star Chamber 23-4
Crump, William 46, 91, *91*
Crump's Apple 91

Day Hours, The 83, 84
Denne, Catherine 25-36, *26*, *27*, 48, 50, 57, 63
Denys, Eleanor 8
Dickens, Charles 28
Digby, Lord 16
Disraeli 82, 87, 88-9

earldom, creation of 29-30
Edinburgh 41
Egiocke, Mary 11
Elgar, Edward 95, 96
    Frank 95, 102
Eliot, Lady Susan Caroline 56
Elizabeth, Queen 8
English Folk dance Society 97
Ernest Augustus, Duke of Cumberland
    & Ernest I of Hanover 54-5

Federation of Australia 105
First World war 112-4
free trade 113
French Revolution 30
friars 5, 6, 7
Frye, Corpl. Solomon 56

Garlicke, Dr. 48
George III 28
Gladstone 88
Glasgow 38-9
Glencoe 42
Gosse, Edmund 113
Grevell, Margery 7
Grey, Earl 114
Grocers Livery Company 13-15, 17, 19
Grosvenor, Lady Lettice 107, *107*, 109
Gyles, Rev. 22
Gylham, Thomas 8

Hallow Park 21
Hanley Castle 9
Hanmer, Susanna 22
Hardie, Keir 110
Hardy, Gathorne 88
Harewell, Elizabeth 9
Heath, Nicholas 8
Henry, Lord Berkeley 8
Hepburn-Stuart-Forbes-Trufusis, Walter 97
Home Rule 101, 110-3
Hornyold, Ralph 9
Howard, Mgr. 86-7

Howells, W.D. 107-9

Izard, Richard 13

Jennens, William 22, 24, 28
Johnson, Dr. Samuel 41

Keble, John 84-5
Kempley Church *118*, 119
Knightley, Samuel 10-11

Landsdowne, Marquess of 113
Landsdowne Letter, the 113-4
Lear, Sidney 85
Lechmere, Anthony 17
Liddon, Canon H.P. 76, 78, 84
Lisle, Bridget 11
Little Stamford, Lincs. 64
Lloyd George 116, 120
Longford, second earl 34
Lower Woodsfield 3
Lucy, Francis 14
Lygon, Anne 7
    Anne (dau. of William the colonel) 11-12
    Corbyn 17-18, 19-20
    Edmund 11
    Edward, General 29, 57, 65
    Edward Hugh ('Eddie'; son of 6th earl) 93, *96*, 102, 104
    Edward Pyndar 34-5, *44*
    Elizabeth the younger 10
        the elder 10
    Felicia 60, 61-5, 66, 69
    Fernando 8
    Frederick, 6th earl 57, 60, 66, 75, 76, 77-92, *82*, *89*, 99
    Georgiana (dau. of 1st earl) 34
    Georgiana (dau. of 4th earl) 60, 65, 70, 77, 78, 85, 86
    Henry, General, 4th earl 29, 34, 43, 53-68
    Henry, 5th earl 60, 69-76, *72*, 85, 86
    Hugh 9
    John, (son of 1st earl) 29
    John Reginald (Lygon) Pindar, 3rd earl 49-52, 73
    Louisa, Lady 36, 43, 44, 45, 46, 66
    Margaret, (dau. of the Correspondent) 21, *21*
    Mary, Lady (née Stanhope) 79, 80, *80*
    Mary, Lady (dau. of 6th earl) 93-8; *94*, 99, 102, 104, 107, 117
    Ralph 8
    Richard 5
    Richard (son of Anne) 7
    Richard (son of William) 9
    Richard (son of the colonel) 12
    Susan, Lady (see also Eliot) 57, 60, 61, 78
    Thomas 4, 5
    Thomas II 11, 14
    William (grandson of Isabel de Bracy) 4
    William (son of Richard) 6
    William 'the Wasteful' 10
    William III (son of 'the Wasteful') 9-10, *9*
    William IV (the colonel) 11
    William the Correspondent 11, 13-18
    William (son of the Correspondent) 17
    William (son of Corbyn) 21, *21*
    William, 1st earl 25-36, *33*
    William, 2nd earl 29, 32
    William, 7th earl 92, 99-120, *101*, *103*, *110*
        as Governor od New South Wales 102-6
        as politician 109-119
        as artist 116-9
    William, 8th earl 121-4
Lygon Almshouses 36, *36*

Macaulay 79
Madresfield 1, 3, 7, 92
    churches 73-6, *73*, *75*, 93
    Court *3*, 10, 11, 29, *51*, *61*, *62*, *63*, 91, 108-9, 122-3
    Grape 91
Manisty, Mrs. Margaret 25
Marks, Eliza 56, 60-6, 69, 77, 78
    Susan 65, 77
Middleton, Charles 28
Mount Argus, Dublin 67, 68
Mountjoy, Mr. 19
Munn, Rev. G.S. 76

Neale, Rev. J.M. 82
New South Wales 102-6
Newland 3, 52, 77, *78*, *79*
Norfolk, duke of (plot) 8
North America, visiting 70-2

Oban 39
Okes, Mr. 81
Oxford Movement 60, 85

Pakenham, Charles 63, 66-8, 86
Passionist Order 66
Payne, Henry 116, 117

Pitt, William 28
Playdell, Elizabeth 10
Preedy, Frederick 75, 77
Puget, Lord Clarence 88
Pugin, Augustus 73, 75
Pusey, Dr. E.B. 78, 84
Pyndar/Pindar, Mary 20
    Sir Paul 20
    Paul 20
    Reginald 20
    Reginald (younger) 21
    Reginald Lygon 22

Reformation, the 8
Rock Garden, the 91
Romans 1
Roxburghe Club 97
Russell, Anne 12
    Mary 9

St. Mary's Church 3
Salisbury, Lord 89-90
Salvation Army 100
Scotland, travels in 38-41
Scott, Lady Charlotte 49, 52
    Col. Charles 52
Shadrach 65
Sharpe, Cecil 94, 96
Simmonds, Augustine 7
Sinclair, Sir John 29
Sladen, Hugh 100
Smyth, Miles 9
South Sea Bubble 16
Staffa 39
Stanhope, Edward 101
    Lord Philip 79
Strontian 42

Teck, Countess of 94
Thomas (a groom) 37
Townsend, Francis 28
Tractarians 82
Tuckfield, Roger 17
    Thomas 14, 16
Tullie, Isaac 20
    Jane 18, 20

University of London 115-6
Urse d'Abitot 2

Victoria, Queen 53, 54, 81

Wakefield, Miss 94
Waldo, Isaac 18, 19
Walsh, Mr. (tutor) 37
Walwen/Walweyn, Robert 9
Waterloo Oak, the 58
Webb, Sidney & Beatrice 110
Wellington, Duke of 79
Wells, H.G. 110
Weston, Arthur T. 79
Winnington-Ingram, Bishop 83
Worcester 92
    Cathedral 2, 5, 6

Also from Logaston Press

Churches of Worcestershire
by Tim Bridges   ISBN 1 873827 56 3   £12.95

Introductory chapters tell of the spread of Christianity across Worcestershire and detail the early development of churches. The major events that affected church building in the county—from new architectural fashions to political upheavals—are detailed to provide a background to the gazetteer that follows. Likewise a history of the changes in internal layout, and of the architects and craftsmen involved in furnishing, design, carving and stained glass is given.

The core of the book is a gazetteer to the Anglican churches of Worcestershire—some 270 in total—allowing this book to be used as a guide when exploring the county. Each entry places the church in its setting, describes the church, gives its building history and details the main decorations, monuments, glass and any notable external features such as lychgates and crosses. As such it is an invaluable aid to explaining what you are seeing—and for ensuring that you don't miss anything on your visit.

Tim Bridges lectures widely on church architecture and history and has gathered together a wealth of information in this book. He works as Collections Manager for Worcester City Museums and has lived in Worcestershire for many years. He also serves as a trustee for the Worcestershire and Dudley Historic Churches Trust, which will financially benefit from the sale of each copy of this book.

With over 140 illustrations.

In Our Dreaming and Singing
The Story of the Three Choirs Festival Chorus
by Barbara Young   ISBN 1 873827 31 8   £6.95

In this book, Barbara Young, for several years a member of the Three Choirs Festival Chorus, explores the origins of that chorus and how it changed to meet the demands of musical taste through three centuries.

This is not a 'dry' book, but a very personal account which will appeal to listeners and singers alike. The story is told from the inside by one who has enjoyed the challenge of learning the greatest works of the choral repertoire, has known the problems posed by new pieces, rehearsed under difficult conditions and felt the excitement and exhilaration of taking part in some memorable performances.

To help tell the tale, the author uses letters and anecdotes from chorus members past and present, and has included many engravings, drawings and photographs.

Also from Logaston Press

Radnorshire from Civil War to Restoration
A study of the county and its environs 1640-60 in a regional setting
by Keith Parker   ISBN 1 973827 86 5 (Pbk) £12.95   ISBN 1 873827 96 2 (Hbk) £18.95

Whilst this book is a record of the social, political, religious and military state of affairs in Radnorshire from before the Civil War to the Restoration, by its nature much reference is made to events in neighbouring counties and further afield. Many of those affecting the course of events in Radnorshire had a base elsewhere, and the military almost universally operated from outside the county.

Keith Parker has made much use of primary sources of information to confound the generally held view that Radnorshire was both a poor county at the time of the Civil War and essentially Royalist in outlook. A more confusing picture emerges of strongly held views by a few on each side, though most notably the pro-Parliamentarians, in a sea of neutrality, bewilderment and opportunism.

This is a story of Radnorshire gentry, farmers and clergymen caught up in an age of both danger and vibrant political and religious debate, when many had a rare chance to shape the future.

Keith Parker, a native of Kington and graduate of Birmingham and London Universities, lives in Presteigne where he was formerly deputy head of John Beddoes School. For many years he has lectured on local history for the Extra-mural Department of the University of Wales, Aberystwyth, and for the Workers' Educational Association. 1997 saw the publication of his popularly acclaimed *A History of Presteigne*, also published by Logaston Press.

The Gale of Life
Essays in the History and Archaeology of South-West Shropshire
ISBN 1 873827 36 9   £6.95

This book comprises twenty essays by a variety of authors with a shared enthusiasm for the history and archaeology of the area. The essays cover Iron Age hillforts, Saxon developments, Offa's Dyke, Roman settlements and roads, the arrival of the Normans, border unrest, vernacular architecture, the Civil War, transport, enclosure, the Community College and much besides.

Published by South-West Shropshire Historical and Archaeological Society in association with Logaston Press.

Also from Logaston Press

Ludlow Castle
Its History & Buildings
Edited by Ron Shoesmith & Andy Johnson   ISBN 1 873827 51 2   £14.95

Ludlow Castle has often played a pivotal role in the history of the Welsh Marches, indeed of the whole of the United Kingdom.

Commenced about 1075 to help control the Welsh border, it became the power base of the de Lacys whose importance escalated on the demise of the fitzOsbern earls of Hereford. The castle became the focus of much bickering for control in the Anarchy, leading to its capture by King Stephen. Subsequently it passed to the de Genevilles, staunch allies of both Edward I and II. When they died without male issue, the castle passed by marriage to the Mortimers. They had risen to prominence under Roger de Mortimer who ruled England as Regent with Edward II's widowed queen, Isabella. The Mortimer family's fortune ebbed and flowed thereafter, their caput being Wigmore Castle, a short distance to the south-west. On the death of Edmund Mortimer in 1425, the Mortimer inheritance passed to Richard, duke of York who was married to Edmund's sister. Ludlow became a favoured residence, and his eldest sons Edward and Edmund spent much their youth at Ludlow. Indeed, on the death of their father at the Battle of Wakefield in the Wars of the Roses, it was from Ludlow that Edward marched to victory at Mortimer's Cross, a few miles to the south, and then advanced on London where he claimed the throne as Edward IV. Ludlow and its castle flourished under its Royal lords. In later years this continued under the Council in the Marches of Wales which lasted from 1534 (when it gained added prestige under Bishop Rowland Lee) to 1689. It was one of the last Royalist garrisons to surrender in the Civil War, was on the point of being used as a PoW camp in the Napoleonic Wars, might have been about to be demolished to make way for a country house, and became a focus of the Picturesque. It still draws devotees.

The buildings themselves are complex, the keep most notably so, with the changes in the structure open to interpretation. Stone built from the beginning, what is now known as the keep started life as an unusual entrance tower. It has undergone extensions, contractions, additions and alterations, during which time the entrance was moved to an adjoining gateway. Towards the end of the 1200s the outer bailey was enclosed in stone, and a new entrance made to the castle which faced east, instead of south, to link directly with the expanding town on the crest of the hill, as opposed to the presumably earlier settlement of Dinham. As the castle's main function moved from that of a castle to that of a royal palace, so it was improved and modernised, and extensively so during the period of the the Council in the Marches of Wales, continuing in use when many of its contemporaries were starting to fall into disrepair.

This book aims to draw together the history of the buildings and its owners to provide a developing picture of the castle and its role in both border and national history and to interpret the changes that occurred in the buildings themselves.

With over 125 colour and black and white illustrations.

Also from Logaston Press

The Herefordshire School of Romanesque Sculpture
by Malcolm Thurlby ISBN 1 873827 60 1 £12.95

This highly illustrated book serves as both a Guide to the surviving work of the Herefordshire School, and provides a history of the school itself.

It compares the surviving work, both in stone and other materials, in Herefordshire, Gloucestershire, Worcestershire and beyond, with that of other styles both at home and abroad—Celtic motifs, Romano-British and Anglo-Saxon work, as well as sculpture in France and Spain.

The sources of inspiration are considered. Clearly the Bible provides some, but by no means all. *The Bestiary*, the Book of Beasts, provides others. Derived from Greek sources translated into Latin, this book described the nature and/or habits of many creatures, both real and fantastic, and reflected on the world of mankind in the realm of nature. The earliest surviving copy of this book is dated *c*.1120, and a copy appears to have used by the patrons of the Herefordshire School.

The book, therefore, also considers who the patrons were and their motives. It looks at the training of the sculptors and their role in the building work, and considers whose hands may have been at work on which sites.

The Herefordshire School of Romanesque Carving is an attempt to bring together the people behind the work, both patrons and carvers, with the architectural and sculptural styles in order to provide a comprehensive picture of the whole.

Contains over 240 illustrations.

Saints in Herefordshire
by D.M. Annett ISBN 1 873827 26 1 £4.95

This book started as a supposedly simple task of listing all the dedications of Herefordshire churches, together with a note on the life of each saint. It proved to be much less straight forward than expected, as more and more churches were found to have had their dedications changed at some unspecified date. What has therefore emerged is a picture of dedications sometimes changing with ecclesiastical fashion, and sometimes through disuse and the often mistaken attempts of 18th-century antiquarians to recover them.

Herefordshire is peculiar amongst English counties, along with Cornwall, in having many churches dedicated to Celtic saints, and brief biographies of these, as well as of biblical and legendary saints, are included. The illustrations (with one exception) are taken from stained glass in churches in the diocese of Hereford.

It is hoped that this book can be enjoyed by anyone with an interest in Herefordshire's history and its churches, while a wealth of reference material has been provided for those who want to delve more deeply into the subject.